PUT YOUR
BEST FOOT FORWARD

SOUTH
AMERICA

PUT YOUR
BEST FOOT FORWARD

SOUTH
AMERICA

*A Fearless
Guide to
International
Communication
and Behavior*

MARY
MURRAY
BOSROCK

IES
International Education Systems

Published by International Education Systems.

Publisher's Cataloging-in-Publication Data

Bosrock, Mary Murray.
      Put your best foot forward—South America: a fearless
  guide to international communication and behavior/
  Mary Murray Bosrock.—1st ed.
      p. cm.— (Put your best foot forward; bk. 5.)
      Includes bibliographical references and index.
      ISBN 0-9637530-8-8
      Preassigned LCCN: 97-71673
      1. South America—Guidebooks. 2. South America —
  Social life and customs. I. Title. II. Series: Bosrock, Mary
  Murray. Put your best foot forward; bk. 5.

      F2211.B67 1997   918.0439
                                   QBI97-40472

Printed in the United States of America
10 9 8 7 6 5 4 3 2 1

To Matt and Steve,

Who have taken

our interest in

this new world

one step further.

With all my love,

Mom.

ATTENTION: BUSINESSES & SCHOOLS

International Education Systems books are available at special discounts when ordered in bulk for business or educational use. For information, please contact:
International Education Systems
26 East Exchange Street, Suite 313
St. Paul, MN 55101
tel. 612/227-2052; Fax 612/223-8383
E-mail: IESpybff@aol.com

Look for other international education products from IES, including:

Put Your Best Foot Forward — *Asia*
Put Your Best Foot Forward — *Europe*
Put Your Best Foot Forward — *Russia*
Put Your Best Foot Forward — *Mexico/Canada*

Illustration: Craig MacIntosh
Design: Brett Olson
Research: Sarah Page
Production: Catherine Walker

TABLE OF CONTENTS

i.

ACKNOWLEDGMENTS

My thanks to the dozens of people—
businesspeople, diplomats, scholars and
professionals—who have drawn on their own
experience to contribute ideas to this book, and
especially to those who have helped review the
manuscript. They include:

General
Serge August
Walkyria F. Batista
Gustavo Galdo
Consul and Mrs. Paul R. Heinerscheid
Peter and Jane Lefferts
Dermot Moore
Susan Murray
Tanya L. Newberry
Fred Rovet
Tammy Swanberg
José Torres
Kris Volk

Argentina
Consulate General of Argentina, Chicago
Consulate General of Argentina, Miami
Awalia Acciardi
Rosa Maria Braile
Livia Normandas, Deputy Consul of Argentina, Miami

Hugo Rodriguez, J.P. Morgan
Armando Bessares
Juan Meschini

Bolivia
Embassy of Bolivia, Washington, DC
Consulate General of Bolivia, Chicago
Consulate General of Bolivia, Miami
Dr. Franklin Bustillos
Miriam Escobar
Dr. Jamie R. Escobar, Consul General
Fernando Lazcano
Ricardo Urquidi

Brazil
Consulate General of Brazil, Miami
Consulate General of Brazil, Chicago
Delores Barbosa
Celso Bello
Charlie Clogston
Anna Mazzuchi Freiman
Claudia Majuri
Inah dos Santos
Antonia Ramalho

Chile
Embassy of Chile, Washington, DC
Consulate General of Chile, Chicago
Consulate General of Chile, Miami
Angela Armstrong
Andrea Bell
Veronica Cariaga
Dr. Raúl Cifuentes
Juan Pablo Guarachi
Arturo Herrera
Cynthia Jenkins
Betty Kretschmer
Eduardo A. Ruiz
Miquel Angel Ruz
Ricardo Salazar
Marcela R. Soto

Colombia
Embassy of Colombia, Washington, DC
Consulate General of Colombia, Miami
Nidia E. Algarin
Fidel Cano, Press Attaché
Diana Serpa-Preciado, Vice Consul
Luis F. Suarez
Dr. Fernando Torres, Consul of Colombia, Minnesota

Ecuador
Embassy of Ecuador, Washington, DC
Dr. Jaime Barberis
Elena de Fernandes
Eduardo Viteri
Steve and Debbie Yanda

Paraguay
Embassy of Paraguay, Washington, DC
Consulate General of Paraguay, Miami
Beatrice Basconsello
Jose Luis Coscia Laguardia, Official Consul
Norma Cardozo

Peru
Embassy of Peru, Washington, DC
Consulate General of Peru, Chicago
Javier Castro, Assistant Press Attaché
Sheana Dempsey
Carmen Lewis
Luis A. Sobrevilla M.D.
Julian Torres, Consul General of Peru, Chicago

Uruguay
Embassy of Uruguay, Washington, DC
Consulate General of Uruguay, Miami
Stanley Diesch, Consul General of Uruguay, Minnesota
Christina Nieto
Estela Queirolo Ferrari, Deputy Consul General, Miami
Eduardo Rosenbrock, First Secretary, Embassy of Uruguay

Venezuela
Consulate General of Venezuela, Miami
Dr. Gustavo Rodríguez-Amengual, Consul General
José Hernandez, Press Attaché
Josefina Sanchez Medina
Brian Potter
Patrick Ritter

Editing Assistance
Shannon Kranz
David Martin

Special thanks to Steve Larson of 3M Company for allowing us to excerpt and paraphrase the e-mail tips in Strictly Business.

A special thank you for the major contributions of Anna Mazzuchi Freiman and Claudia Majuri, two beautiful Brazilian women, and Armando Bessares, a charming gentleman from Argentina.

And to all the South Americans who love their countries so much—for your time and help, my sincere thanks.

—*Mary Murray Bosrock*
Saint Paul, Minnesota
Spring 1997

ii.

INTRODUCTION

This book is not about manners and it is not about etiquette. This book is about survival—for our companies, for our economy and for our way of life that they support.

This book is about survival.

The global economy is a reality today. World economies are integrating far faster than anyone projected. Shortly, every business in every country will be affected by globalization.

To survive, we must be able to compete in this truly global economy. To compete effectively, we must understand more about other countries, other cultures, and other ways of doing business.

There was a time when such intercultural understanding was a nicety, a luxury for a select few. No longer. The world has changed dramatically.

For nearly forty years after World War II, the United States was the world's preeminent military, political and economic power. We were the unchallenged leader of the Free World and, with rare exceptions, we got what we wanted.

That began to change more than a decade ago with the emergence of Germany and Japan as economic superpowers. The change continued with the rapid industrialization of several countries on the Pacific Rim and accelerated with the end of the Cold War and the dissolution of the Soviet Union.

Suddenly, we find ourselves in a global arena in which strategic military power is less important than economic power, and in which we are only one of several major players—the largest, to be sure, but by no means dominant.

Everyone accepts the reality of interdependence.

As much as we may yearn for the good old days, it's unlikely in the foreseeable future that any country will dominate world affairs and the world economy as the United States did in the years after the Second World War.

We need to make up our minds that we can and will compete successfully in this new, interdependent global economy. That means understanding our potential customers and competitors and the cultures in which they're rooted.

Everyone accepts the reality of interdependence. The challenge is to understand how that reality affects each of us, our companies and the ways we do business abroad.

Put Your Best Foot Forward—South America
covers the major economies in South America.
It is written for those doing business in or
visiting the major metropolitan areas. Every
country in South America has its own ancient
culture, each rich in history, art, language, food,
music and tradition. I encourage you to explore
these treasures. However, this book does not
attempt to describe the beauty and richness of
South American cultures. Rather, it is a guide
for communicating with South Americans.

Only countries with major populations are
included in this book—our apologies to
Guyana, Suriname, the Falkland Islands and
French Guiana. If you are visiting countries not
covered in this book, refer to the general
guidelines for South America found in Part Two.

*This book is
written as a
first step.*

I present to you the following materials as a
general guide—a way of showing your South
American colleagues that you care to know
them. This book is written as a first step in
what I hope will become a wonderful
opportunity for you to become friends with
some of the warmest and most interesting
people in the world.

FORMAT

Everyone who reads this book is busy. I've
attempted to respect your time by organizing
the book into easily accessible sections divided
by country and by behavior. These quick-

reference chapters give you a snapshot of each country that allows you to find the information you need easily.

WHO SHOULD USE THIS BOOK?

Although it was designed primarily as a resource for business people, this book should be equally helpful for leisure travelers, students, teachers, people in the travel and hospitality industry, and hosts who regularly entertain South American visitors.

Keep this book on your desk or tuck it in your suitcase. Before you meet or talk with someone from South America you can quickly learn or review important facts that will assist you in communicating clearly.

STAYING AT HOME

You needn't travel abroad to find this information important and useful for your day-to-day life. Increasingly, people who never leave the United States need international skills. In New York City alone there are more than 143 newspapers and magazines, 22 television stations and 12 radio stations writing and speaking in more than 30 languages.

A cotton farmer in Georgia tracks the weather daily in the cotton growing region in China. If the Chinese have poor cotton growing weather, he plants a double crop. A New York banker transfers millions of dollars to

Argentina within seconds by simply touching a button on a computer.

Since the beginning of its nationhood, the United States has been predominately a Western European culture. However, by the year 2010, more than half of the U.S. population will have roots outside of Western Europe.

In 1996, people of Latin American heritage made up ten percent of the U.S. population of 266.5 million people. African Americans made up 12 percent, Asians contributed 3.3 percent, and whites accounted for 73 percent of the population.

It is estimated that in the year 2050, the percentage of the population from Latin American heritage (from Central and South America and the Caribbean) will increase to 26 percent of a U.S. population likely to be in excess of 400 million people.

Forty million United States residents are foreign born. Your boss, your next door neighbor, your child's best friend, your juror, your patient, your client, your customer or a student in your classroom may be from another country. These citizens spend billions annually—not a market to be ignored!

Forty million United States residents are foreign born.

KNOCK KNOCK

A North American fifth grade teacher told me about a South American boy who visited her class for four weeks. Because of an appointment one morning, he arrived at school late. He stood in the hall and knocked on the door. No one heard him, so he knocked again. Finally, after several knocks, the teacher went to the door and to her surprise the little lad was in tears. To make things worse, the children all laughed and said, "Dummy, you don't knock on the classroom door!" The little boy explained that where he came from, one never enters a room without knocking. Those children who laughed could have used a lesson in politeness and manners—certainly the most important components of international communication.

THE BOTTOM LINE

The information in this book isn't just "nice to know." It's vital to your success and that of your company if you want to do business in South America or with South Americans. The information in this book can be translated into increased revenues and earnings for your company. What you learn in this book will literally go to the bottom line.

iii.

CONSIDERATION

Consideration and respect are the qualities you need most to be a successful internationalist. Every behavior presented in this book is, in essence, considerate and thoughtful. It is so easy! You can't go wrong if you always ask yourself, "Are my actions considerate?"

Most dictionaries define *considerate* as "having regard for the needs or feelings of others." The word was derived from *consider,* one definition of which is "to examine, study, deliberate upon."

It's clear in this context that examining, studying and preparing are what consideration is all about. You can't be considerate of others—especially in another culture—without taking the time to learn.

Doing your homework before you visit a new country is essential, but once you're on the ground, there are important ways to keep learning. Here are some of them:

> *"Consideration for others separates the savage from the civilized man."*
>
> *–Emily Post*

Observe what the local people are doing. This is one of the safest and easiest ways to establish appropriate behavior. Quietly watch what others wear, how they greet each other, how they eat. Follow their behavior and you will usually be correct.

Ask whenever communication or expected behavior is unclear. Ask your host or business associate, the concierge at the hotel, a clerk in a shop. Ask quietly and politely. You may feel foolish at first, but people always appreciate that you're trying to learn.

Here are the kinds of things you'll want to ask if they're not absolutely clear:

- What is the expected attire for an event?

- What is the proper pronunciation of a name?

"You see but you don't observe."

–Sherlock Holmes

- What tip is expected?

- What is an appropriate gift for an occasion?

- What is the proper way of wrapping and presenting a gift?

- What flowers are appropriate for an occasion?

- When and where may I smoke?

- What time does an invitation *really* mean?

Whenever there are ambiguities—linguistic or otherwise—ask politely for clarification. It's much better to ask a question than to risk misunderstanding.

Listen actively and aggressively. Write down what you hear. When a person says his or her name, listen carefully to the pronunciation. Write down the phonetic pronunciation of the name. Listen for the title used.

In meetings or presentations listen intently to what your hosts are saying and take careful notes. You're sending them a signal that you're taking them seriously.

If people are speaking in English as a courtesy to you, remember that they may be speaking in their second or third language. This may require a little extra listening effort on your part. If you get impatient, just think about how well you'd be expressing yourself in your second or third language.

At social functions, pay careful attention to what local people are saying to you and to each other. You'll learn a lot about the country and culture that will come in handy in future conversations, and you'll have many opportunities to ask informed questions. Genuine interest is always appreciated.

It's much better to ask a question than to risk misunderstanding.

Genuine interest is always appreciated.

You can learn a lot about appropriate behavior by observing, asking and listening. Especially in another culture, the ultimate learning technique is trial and error. You've got to be willing to try new things, and you've got to be willing to make your share of errors.

Try to speak a few words of someone's language, taste the local food, greet people properly, learn others' behaviors, and you'll already be a success. To try is to show your vulnerability, your humanity.

Believe me, trying covers a multitude of errors! We make mistakes when communicating in our own culture, so we certainly cannot expect to be perfect when communicating in someone else's. Remember, perfection is boring anyway! You never need to attain perfection—you just need to *try*.

When you try, people understand that you're taking a risk—making a special effort to reach out to them. They give you credit both for being willing to take the risk and for being willing to make the effort.

On such credit are new friendships—and new business relationships—built.

iv.
LETTER FROM SOUTH AMERICA

Over the past several years, as I've collected
material for this book, I've asked a number of
South Americans how they view North America
and what points they'd like to make to North
Americans who visit their countries. The following
letter is a compilation of some of their most
important comments:

Dear Neighbors,

You asked what South Americans think about
our neighbors to the north. Well, the answer is,
we like the United States and its people a great
deal.

We like your willingness to recognize your
problems and discuss them openly. We like your
attempt to provide freedom for everyone. Many
of us, since childhood, have idealized North
American people and what we thought was
your lifestyle. We admire the society and
economy you have created. You are clearly an
economic superpower, and when you come here

to do business, you generally come with excellent products, competitively priced.

However, we would like you much better if you took the time to get to know us, who we are and what we care about. We know so much about you, but you know very little about us.

You are the most powerful economy in the world and leaders in just about everything. But how can you lead if you know nothing about the rest of the world? We know you are proud of your country—and you should be—but please recognize that there is a world south, north, east and west of your borders.

South America has just about every type of landscape and climate. Waterfalls, huge lakes, rocky windswept islands, deserts, snow peaked mountains, rolling grasslands and active volcanoes cover the 6,885,000 square miles of land. The Amazon River Basin, which occupies about two-fifths of the continent, is the world's largest tropical rain forest and is referred to as "the lungs for the world."

Our continent has rich farmlands, vast timberlands and some of the largest and most valuable mineral deposits in the world.

We are creative and intelligent people who have learned to survive despite political and economic instability. Please do not treat us in a demeaning or condescending manner. We are not "underdeveloped." We are very offended when you ask if we have cars and electricity. You are not traveling to prehistoric days if you are visiting or moving to South America. We don't live in trees!

We are not "underdeveloped."

The general stereotype of South America in the U.S. seems to be that all South Americans speak Spanish, have dark hair and dark eyes, and are Catholic. In reality, we are much more diverse than that. Half of the continent was colonized by Portugal. In more recent times, our countries have drawn immigrants in great numbers from all over the world. Today, you will find large communities of Germans, Italians, Japanese and Lebanese, among others, in South America. Our indigenous cultures are rich and vibrant.

We are not all one culture.

The differences are not merely a matter of language, but also of historical and cultural patterns and, most of all, mentality. We are not all one!

We are not interested in knowing whether your background is German, Korean, Italian or Jewish. However, we are very interested in knowing your educational and family background, which will be your screen of acceptance. Money is less a criterion than your attire, social graces, culture (knowledge of geography, history, and fine arts) and pleasant personality. These are the qualities that will allow you acceptance into our elite circles.

If you are a millionaire but act crudely and without social graces, you will never be accepted in higher circles. People who brag about what they have and show off their money embarrass us.

The United States has evolved into an egalitarian society and the power distance is very small between your people. In South America, the classes live separately. Please do not act superior or lecture us on "equality" and "democracy."

We are very interested in politics and discuss it often. In the United States, it makes little difference in your day-to-day life whether the Democrats or the Republicans are in power. This is not true in South America. The differences between the parties are extreme, and who is in power changes the country drastically. This is one reason not to give your opinion on the politics of our countries.

Money is less a criterion for acceptance than your attire, social graces, culture and pleasant personality.

We know how to celebrate life, and we love to dance and party. North Americans may think they can cheat death, but we know better. We take time to enjoy a lunch, a dinner, a party, a person.

We take time to enjoy a lunch, a dinner, a party, a person.

When you invite someone to dinner at 7:00, you not only expect your guests to arrive on time, but you also want them to leave by 9:00. You even write this on your invitations.
Not us. An invitation for a 7:00 party indicates that it probably *starts* at 9:00—and plan to stay until breakfast.

Women are loved in South America. Men are always looking at women! Some men make comments, compliment and flirt with women. South American women are used to it and if they don't like it, they ignore it. If you don't want to be flirted with, say so clearly and firmly—but politely—and men will stop.

We hope we are polite while we are guests in your country, but we do find it difficult to always know what is "politically correct." In South America, men and women compliment each other openly, even in the workplace. We hug and kiss our associates, our friends and especially our children. Women dance with women at parties and we just have fun. We are not sure how this is viewed in the U.S.

With the global community expanding, many of us live in your country. We enjoy living in your cities and believe we make valuable contributions in our work. We carry a green card, which allows us to work in the U.S. But we can't help wondering why the green card is pink and, even worse, why does it refer to us as "resident aliens?" We are from South America, not Mars!

Yes, we enjoy living and working in your country, but please don't say how "lucky" we are to be there instead of home. We love our countries as much as you love yours. While you may have certain material comforts that are not as readily available in our countries, we have very rich lives in South America. We are not as concerned with things as we are with people.

Please visit us. We are very proud of our countries and our cultures. We have some of the most breathtaking landscapes in the world. We are warm and friendly and we'll welcome you with open arms. But please, first take time to learn about who we are.

Respectfully,

Your South American Friends and Neighbors

PART
I

*How To Go
International*

Put Your Best Foot Forward

1.

APPEARANCES CAN BE DECEPTIVE

Just because it seems as though everyone everywhere in the world is wearing Levi's, drinking Coca-Cola and eating Big Macs doesn't mean we are becoming the same. Ask the Austrians if they are becoming like the Germans. Ask the Koreans if they are just like the Japanese and ask the Argentines if they are the same as the Brazilians.

People are not becoming the same; quite the opposite is happening. As political, legal and bureaucratic barriers fall, and people from diverse cultures are being forced to play on the same economic field, a new sense of sacred is evolving. Individual countries are more than ever defending their uniqueness and resisting the loss of "local." They instinctively strive to hang on to their cultural identities.

People are not becoming the same.

Success in the global marketplace does not require an MBA, extensive international experience or a foreign language capability. It does require knowledge of the various symbols, core values, traditions and passions that are important to people.

Business is done between people. Therefore, business relationships begin and develop as personal relationships. You will never completely understand another culture. You can, however, show your potential customers and colleagues that you are not an interloper attempting to "make a killing" in their home, but someone who wants to know them, their country and their culture.

Once the United States was unchallenged. No longer! The new world is charged with challenges and opportunities. Imagine the number of new markets available to you. The old rules will not work in the new game, though. You need to do your homework.

To succeed in the 21st century, you need to be capable of buying and selling in different cultures. A world of opportunity awaits you, if you are willing to make the effort.

2.
NEVER GENERALIZE

Each of the world's six billion people is a unique individual. People cannot be stereotyped. It is particularly difficult to say anything in general about South America—a continent that has mountains, glaciers, jungles, fjords, beaches, deserts, and plains; a continent that is inhabited by Native Americans, Spanish, Portuguese, Germans, Italians, English, Japanese and Lebanese.

People cannot be stereotyped.

That's what makes going international so much fun! Even though people may look alike, speak the same language, eat similar food, attend the same church and live in the same country, each and every person you meet will be different.

Just about the time you're tempted to put labels on people, you'll meet a gregarious Finn, a humorless Irishman, an inhibited Italian, a rude Japanese, a lethargic German or an unfriendly Brazilian, and all your rules will go right out the window. So never, never, never generalize!

I have been in homes, shops, offices and embassies with people of the same nationality and listened to them debate a particular custom or behavior. Women disagreed with men, older people disagreed with younger ones, and sometimes there was general disagreement. Only rarely did such a group reach consensus.

Trying to describe human behavior is tricky at best. No two people behave in exactly the same way; perhaps more important, no two people interpret others' behavior in the same way.

No two people behave in exactly the same way.

Does this make intercultural communication impossible for the ordinary business traveler? Certainly not! Although you'll probably never meet a Bolivian or Chilean with all of the qualities I describe, after a quarter century of experience and years of research, I feel comfortable in saying that in general there are certain qualities, customs and characteristics you'll encounter when dealing with people from a particular country.

Can you survive without this knowledge? Of course you can. Can this information help you to understand and feel more comfortable with South Americans? Can it help you to avoid misunderstanding? Can it help you to communicate clearly and effectively? You bet it can!

Exotic places and the sights and activities they offer have been the subject of hundreds of travel books, but relatively little has been written about the people who live in these places and how we can relate to them.

This book is an attempt to make your interaction with South Americans easier, more comfortable and more fun. It is intended to get you over some of the first cultural hurdles so you can establish productive business relationships—and, I hope, friendships as well.

It is the people who hold my interest and win my heart.

There isn't a country I've worked or traveled in that I haven't enjoyed. And regardless of how dynamic the business environment or how beautiful the countryside, it is always the people—tens and hundreds and thousands of people—who hold my interest and eventually win my heart.

Put Your Best Foot Forward

3.
THE TEN COMMANDMENTS OF VISITING SOUTH AMERICA

1. Recognize and respect uniqueness. Each country and each person within the country is unique.

2. Do your homework. A basic knowledge of each country's culture and history will be richly rewarded.

3. Make the effort to build relationships.

4. Never compare countries with each other or with your country.

5. Never pass judgment on the political or social system of another country.

6. Take your time and be patient. The pace of life and business may be very different from your country.

7. Be flexible. Adapt to the environment you are in. Do not expect others to adapt to your style.

Always be sincere. It shows.

8. Always be sincere. It shows.

Assume the best about people and their actions.

9. Ask, look and listen! South Americans are proud of their culture and history. They will enjoy teaching you about their ways.

10. Assume the best about people and their actions. Most behavior is rational once we understand the rationale.

4.
THE TOP TEN BLUNDERS
OF VISITING SOUTH AMERICA

BLUNDER #1

"I'm from America."

South Americans are "Americans" too. They
are very offended when this fact is ignored!
Refer to yourself as a "North American" and
your country as "the United States."

BLUNDER #2

South Americans are Hispanic.

South Americans do not use the word
"Hispanic." It is a creation from the United
States that is not appreciated by South
Americans. And not only is the word incorrect,
it is inaccurate. The majority of South
Americans are not of Spanish descent.

BLUNDER #3

South America is an underdeveloped region.

The economies in South America may be developing, but they are not "underdeveloped," nor are the countries. How would you like to be referred to as "underdeveloped"? The word is insulting and condescending.

BLUNDER #4

Burp, Slurp, Smack!

South Americans have and appreciate refined manners. If you hope to make friends, watch your table manners.

BLUNDER #5

"Aren't you lucky to be working in the United States?"

South Americans love their countries as much as you love yours. In fact, some South Americans working in the United States get special "hardship pay," particularly those who live in some of the harsher climates of the U.S.

BLUNDER #6

"Just sign the contract, I'm in a hurry!"

Business in South America is
based on relationships.
Relationships take time to
build. If you rush, you almost
certainly will go home
empty-handed.

BLUNDER #7

"A kiss—ugh! I hate any body contact!"

South American people are very warm and
friendly. They will give you a kiss on your
cheek once they get to know you. To reject this
offer of warmth would be unthinkably rude.

BLUNDER #8

"The invitation said 7:00. I'll be right on time."

7:00 may mean 7:30, 8:00, 8:30—but never
7:00! If you arrive "on time," be prepared to
find your host in the shower. When in doubt,
ask a colleague what time is appropriate for a
particular function.

BLUNDER #9

"Coffee? No thanks, I hate coffee!"

This is not a time to say "no thanks." Coffee is king in many South American countries. Remember that coffee built a number of South American cities.

BLUNDER #10

"I'm a vegetarian. I never touch meat!"

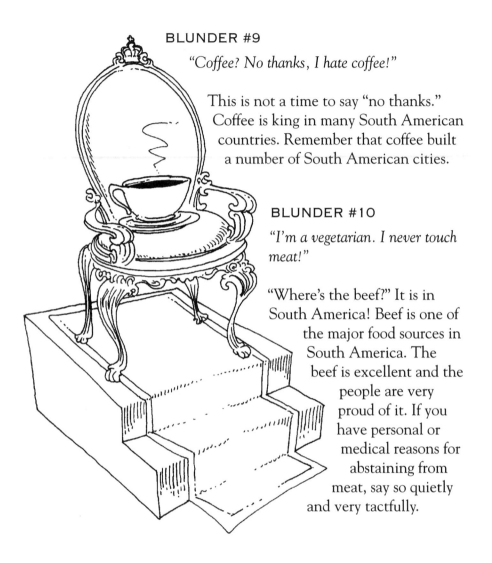

"Where's the beef?" It is in South America! Beef is one of the major food sources in South America. The beef is excellent and the people are very proud of it. If you have personal or medical reasons for abstaining from meat, say so quietly and very tactfully.

5.

WHO ARE SOUTH AMERICANS?

South Americans are our neighbors. While we have a great deal in common, we are also very different. The people who settled North America did so to flee oppression and relinquish their old ways. This was not true of the original settlers of South America. The Spaniards and Portuguese who emigrated from the Old World considered themselves part of their mother countries and kept their traditions.

The societies they formed in South America were based on the lifestyle of the European countries from which they came. The lifestyle of Europe was based on status. Status was based on birth and bloodlines. People learned to be loyal to individuals, not to laws or a constitution.

Many of the Europeans who came to South America—from colonial times to the present day—did so in order to take advantage of the economic opportunities and natural resources

THE PEOPLE

Love thy neighbor.

You may visit an Argentine businessman and be greeted by a fellow in a loden jacket who speaks German.

of the region. Many came with money, bought land, started businesses and became wealthy. They may have felt no need to adapt to the local cultures. That is why today you may visit an Argentine businessman and be greeted by a fellow in a loden jacket who speaks German.

Approximately three-fourths of South Americans are city dwellers, making this one of the most urban continents. City life is fast paced and cities are the centers of political, economic and intellectual life, with varieties of cultural and recreational activities.

DIVERSITY

South Americans share a common colonial heritage, but have great local differences. Differences depend largely upon the ethnic make-up of the people—African, American Indian or European heritage—and different geography and economic developments.

Half of the South American population lives in Brazil and speaks Portuguese.

You might think that one common denominator among South Americans is that most people speak Spanish. Wrong! Half of the South American population lives in Brazil and speaks Portuguese. There are communities of indigenous people, as well as Japanese, Lebanese, Germans and others, who speak their native languages.

Initially, most Europeans hailed from Spain or Portugal. However, there has been robust immigration from Britain, France, Germany,

Italy, the Netherlands and Poland—to name only a few.

In some ways, South America is more diverse than the United States. Immigrants from other lands have been welcomed and have become successful leaders while maintaining unique communities with their own people.

South America is at least as diverse as the United States.

- The president of Peru, Alberto Fujimori, is the son of a Japanese immigrant.

- Argentina has a first-generation Syrian president, Carlos Menem.

- Brazil has the largest Japanese population in the world outside of Japan.

- Brazil has more Lebanese residents than Lebanon.

- There is an area in Venezuela, Colonia Tovar, where all the blond, blue-eyed residents speak only German—and have done so for generations.

- Americana, just outside São Paulo, Brazil, is a community founded by Confederate refugees after the U.S. Civil War.

"SALUD"

In Chile they will ask you "Where else in the world can you find German immigrants who speak Spanish and revere a national hero named O'Higgins?" It has been said that Argentines are Spanish-speaking people who consider themselves English and think they live in Paris.

Most Indians and blacks are fiercely proud of their heritage. Many are more proud of their ethnic group or tribe than their country.

VALUE SYSTEMS

In South America, a person is valued for his or her uniqueness.

INDIVIDUALITY

The word *individual* has a very different meaning in South America than in North America.

North American people tend to define themselves and decide who they are by what they *do* and/or *accomplish* in their lives—this is often determined by what career or occupation a person chooses.

In South America, a person is valued for his or her *uniqueness*. This carries through every aspect of life in South America. People and relationships will always be valued more than schedules or deadlines.

When you're doing business in South America, Arthur Andersen can help you take great strides toward global success.

Whether it's helping you solve the corporate complexities of doing business in South America or helping your employees and their families deal with everyday life in a foreign country, Arthur Andersen is ready.

We've helped companies establish or expand operations in South America for more than 40 years. We can help you with myriad tax issues such as international tax planning, licensing, individual and corporate compliance, acquisitions and joint ventures. In addition, we can serve your human resource needs, including developing and administering international compensation and benefits policies and outsourcing human resource and expatriate services.

Our experienced professionals are part of our worldwide network of nearly 400 offices in 79 countries, sharing centralized training and a common methodology to assure you high standards and continuity of service throughout the world.

All of which will help you take giant steps toward reaching your goals. Visit us on the Internet at http://www.arthurandersen.com.

John Mott, Partner in charge
International Tax and Business Advisory Services
212-708-6012

Mac Gajek, Partner in charge
International Executive Services
312-507-6810

ARTHUR
ANDERSEN

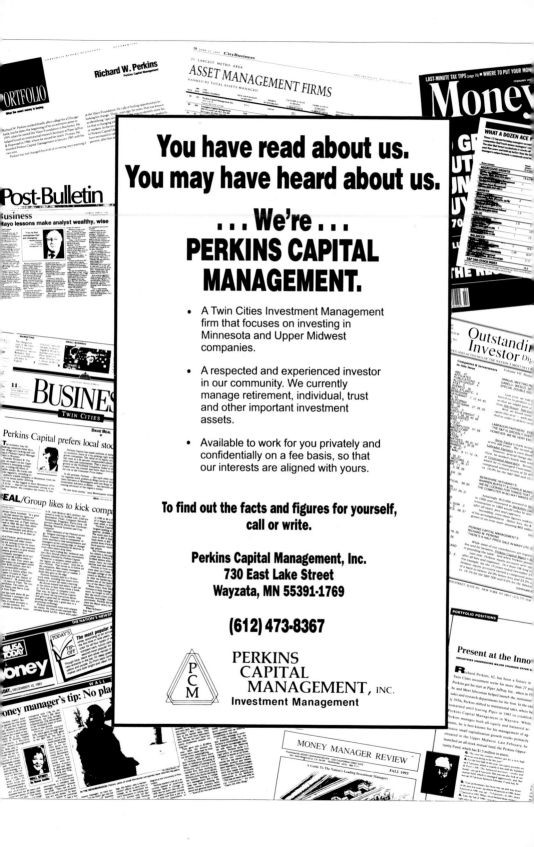

CLASS

You cannot discuss South America without talking about class. You may not feel comfortable or agree with the class structures, but as a guest in someone else's country, it is important that you not attempt to impose your values on their lives.

In many South American countries—as in much of the rest of the world—the middle class, upper-middle class and elite live completely apart from the working class. The standard of living in South America varies greatly.

Most elite and upper-middle class South Americans have servants. Most of them are treated very well—almost like part of the family. However, the *almost* is very important. The servants and the family form a relationship where everyone clearly understands their roles. If you are visiting a South American country, you may not understand this relationship, but it is important that you respect it. It will make everyone uncomfortable if, in an attempt to be what you consider kind or egalitarian, you try to develop a personal relationship with the people who work for your host.

Faux Pas

Do not attempt to impose your values on their lives.

Be polite and considerate, but never overly friendly.

A North American woman was visiting the home of a friend in Argentina. After dinner she asked the family to gather together for a picture. Since the woman who served as the maid and nanny had been with them

SMILE

most of the day, the North American asked her to join in the photograph. The maid declined politely but she and the family were obviously embarrassed. The North American woman, trying to be kind, had made everyone uncomfortable.

FAMILY

Family life is very important in South America. Not only parents and children, but grandparents, aunts, uncles and cousins share closeness, loyalty and cooperation. This extended family provides financial help, security and a social life to all its members.

The elderly are highly respected. Older parents live with their children. In elite and upper class homes, a special area is often built onto the family home for the grandparents. Never ignore an older person. Always greet the oldest people in a group first and take time to visit. Give your seat to older people on the bus. It is expected and will be noticed.

The elderly are highly respected.

Of course, the family is revered in every culture in the world. However, there are few cultures in which family loyalties and obligations play such a vital role in people's business and professional lives. Do not underestimate the influence of family in your South American colleagues' lives. It overshadows all professional considerations.

MACHISMO

Most North Americans associate machismo with sexual overtones. However, in South America it is more about being masculine. A "machoman" is confident. He has charisma and is eloquent, charming and witty. He can be tall or short, fat or skinny— appearance doesn't matter. He is in control and no task is impossible for him. Imagine a John Wayne type character. You may like him or you may not like him—but you will meet him in South America!

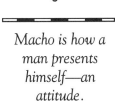

Macho is not necessarily a bad word. Macho is how a man presents himself—an attitude. Macho men believe that they are allowed to do certain things and have certain privileges simply because they are men.

Many South American women accept this and some do like it. However, many younger women, as well as those who are well-educated and traveled, no longer accept this attitude.

Macho is how a man presents himself—an attitude.

THE DRUG PROBLEM

The drug problem is not a South American or a North American problem. This problem belongs to the world. It is the longest-lasting war of the 20th century and has taken hundreds of thousands of lives, robbing the world of its most precious resource: its young people.

There is a great deal of finger-pointing on all sides–North America blames South America for drug production and South America blames North America for drug consumption. Drugs and drug pushers have no regard for national borders. We must work together to disable and destroy every phase of the drug process, from planting, harvesting and processing to transportation, distribution and consumption.

This problem belongs to the world.

Pointing fingers and trying to place blame on others doesn't solve the problem. Every country must join together in this battle, working to help end the greatest threat to world security and stability in our times.

If you are going to South America or working with South Americans, never make a flippant remark about drugs or drug use.

6.

TERMS AND DEFINITIONS

It is important that you understand and use terms accurately to avoid giving offense. Just as there are many words that are "politically incorrect" in the United States, there are words that shouldn't be used or used carefully in South America.

Latin America: the territory covering the Western Hemisphere south of the United States. It includes Mexico, Central America and South America, and is comprised of 33 independent countries and thirteen political units.

South America: The continent is divided into twelve independent countries and two other political units. The independent countries of South America include Argentina, Bolivia, Brazil, Chile, Colombia, Ecuador, Guyana, Paraguay, Peru, Suriname, Uruguay, and Venezuela. The Falkland Islands and French Guiana are dependencies in South America.

There are words that shouldn't be used in South America.

South America is the fourth largest continent in the world in area. It ranks fifth among the continents in population with 318 million people. South America covers about twelve percent or one-eighth of the world's land. South America is almost totally surrounded by water. It borders land only at the Isthmus of Panama, where this narrow strip links Central America with Colombia.

Mestizo: a person of mixed Indian and European descent. Colombia, Paraguay, and Venezuela are comprised mostly of mestizos. Avoid using this term if possible; while some South Americans use it freely, others find it offensive. In some countries, it is used as a demographic term, but never to describe individuals.

Mulatto: a person of mixed black and European descent. Brazil has a large population of mulattos. Again, South Americans may use this word only to describe populations, rather than people. Avoid its use if possible.

Never use the following words, which are inaccurate as well as downright condescending, when referring to South America or South Americans.

- Hispanic

- Underdeveloped

- Banana Republic

Citizens of the United States should be aware of the significance of the words "America" and "American" to many in South America. The word "America," of course, comes from Amerigo Vespucci, the intrepid Italian explorer of the Western Hemisphere. All inhabitants of North, Central, and South America are technically "Americans," and their countries are in "America" as well.

Difficulty arises for those of us from the United States not because we consider ourselves the "only" Americans, but rather that we do not have a distinct English word to describe ourselves. So what should we do?

Although also technically inaccurate, using the term "North American" to refer to citizens of the United States is often seen as less offensive (even though, of course, the term also applies to Mexicans and Canadians). You should also be prepared to use such phrases as "a citizen of the United States."

All that said, the common Spanish terms for citizens of the United States are americanos and norteamericanos. Although a specific word does exist in Spanish to label someone from the United States very accurately—estadounidense—it is more commonly used when writing, not when speaking.

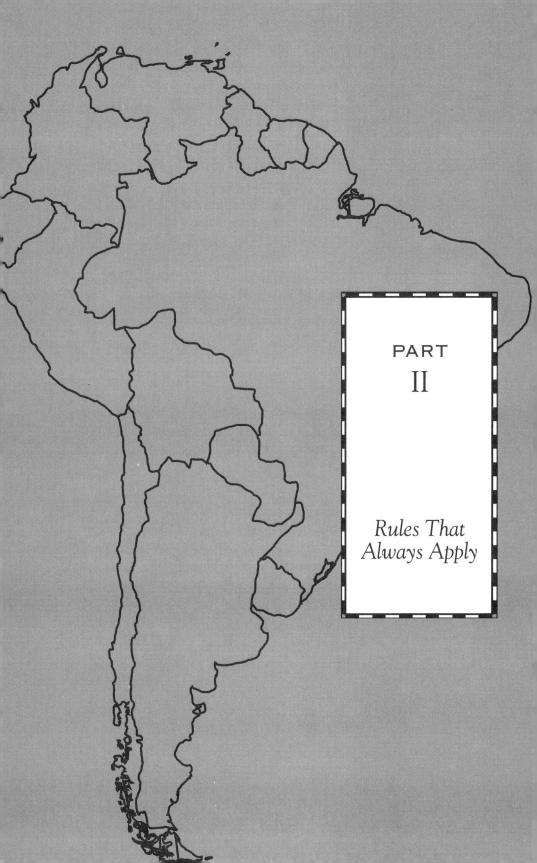

PART
II

*Rules That
Always Apply*

Put Your Best Foot Forward

7.
VITAL STATISTICS

The most frequent negative comment made about North Americans is that they know nothing about people elsewhere, and even worse, don't seem to care to learn.

North Americans are not boors, dummies or ugly. However, North Americans are uninformed and more naive than many people from other cultures.

South America is a continent made up of twelve independent countries. Each of these countries has its own unique culture, history, ethnic make-up, indigenous population, government and traditions.

Each country and its people are distinctly different. They are no more the same than the Australians are like the Canadians, the Koreans are like the Japanese, or the Germans are like the Austrians.

A Brazilian gentleman told me about a well-meaning North American who asked him, "Where are you from?" He responded, "Brazil." "Oh," said the North American, "I have a friend in Chile." The Brazilian thought, "So what? That's like saying to a North American, 'Where do you live?' 'Minnesota.' 'Oh, I have a friend in California.'" Such ignorance, while unintentional, is offensive.

Faux Pas

Not knowing the fundamental facts is not only ignorant but also arrogant.

Isn't it strange that the same business person who spends every weekend trying to figure out how to approach the eighteenth hole on a golf course will travel to another country to negotiate a multi-million dollar deal and never take as much as *one hour* to learn how to approach the people—potential customers and colleagues?

Succeeding in the international arena doesn't require an MBA, foreign language training or cross-border experience. It does require *respect* for the people you deal with. And respect means taking the time to develop a basic knowledge of your hosts' country and the way your hosts live. Not knowing the fundamental facts is not only ignorant but also arrogant.

When visiting a country, you should know the:

• Official name of the country.

- Collective name for its people.

- Primary language(s) spoken.

- President's or prime minister's name.

- Political system.

- Value system.

- Proper means of addressing people.

- Proper gift to give.

- Proper attire to wear.

- Dining habits.

While people in the U.S. are often considered uninformed, people worldwide are equally capable of sensitivity, insensitivity and ignorance.

Ignorance is NOT bliss. Ignorance is offensive.

CHILLY WISHES

The people of Colombia have never forgotten or forgiven former president Ronald Reagan for saying "I'm so pleased to be in Bolivia" when he arrived in Bogotá. This is not a uniquely North American mistake. The president of Portugal arrived in Chile to attend the 1996 Summit of the Americas. In greeting his hosts, he said, "I bring you the warmest wishes from the people of Portugal to the people of the great nation of Cuba." The Chileans laughed but were not amused.

8.
MEETING AND GREETING

The first impression is powerful! A good first impression creates the expectation of a positive relationship. A bad first impression, on the other hand, can be overcome only with a lot of work over a long period of time—and we rarely get that chance.

The moment we meet someone, we judge him or her by what we see and feel. Studies have shown that this process takes less than ten seconds. Whether you begin a good relationship or doom any chance of one can literally depend on the silent signals you send and receive during the first moments of contact.

Greeting is never more important than in South America. Greetings are warm and expressive. Handshakes may be lengthy followed by hugs and embraces (*abrazos*). The time taken with each person is intended to stress that the individual is welcome and recognized. Always personally acknowledge everyone present when entering and leaving a room. Group greetings and farewells are considered a grave offense.

| MODERN MANNERS –NOT! | *A Colombian woman was appalled when visiting a friend in the United States. When she entered her friend's home, the North American woman greeted her warmly, and graciously offered her refreshments. However, during the entire visit, the children in the family never acknowledged her or looked up from the TV even once to say "hello."* |

GENERAL RULES FOR MEETING AND GREETING

Rule of Thumb

Smile!

- Greetings are very important. Never begin a conversation or approach anyone for information until you have greeted him or her properly. Do not shout a greeting from a distance.

- Smile!

- Eye contact is essential when meeting and greeting.

- Greet the most senior person or the head of the family first.

- Shake hands when meeting for the first time. Shake hands with everyone present when arriving and again when leaving a business meeting or a social event. Except at work, men and women always shake hands or kiss each time they meet, even if they have seen each other earlier in the day.

- Be prepared for a lengthy handshake accompanied by warm conversation. Handshakes may be accompanied by a clap on the shoulder and be followed by hugs and embraces. When greeting, most people expect body contact.

- Women should always offer their hands to men.

- Say a personal good-bye to every person when departing.

A KISS IS NOT JUST A KISS

Anyone who has ever been to South America or has become acquainted with South Americans knows that the people are very warm and friendly. Women often kiss each other and male friends twice. Women may even kiss their boss and male colleagues in an office setting when leaving or returning from a holiday, celebrating a birthday or expressing thanks. Men kiss women they are related to, friends with or have met before. Men may also kiss a woman they meet for the first time if she is the wife or daughter of a friend.

This kind of kissing is done between friends, family and business colleagues with whom one

Rule of Thumb

Be expressive—this is not the time or place to be reserved or low key.

has developed a relationship. This greeting is *not* given to a businessperson one has met for the first time, especially in a business setting. If you are meeting a South American for the first time, *do not kiss!*

SMART KISS

A beautiful young Brazilian woman attended a business meeting in a North American company. One of the executives wished to show his colleagues how sophisticated and knowledgeable he was about South America. When he entered the room and was introduced to the woman, he gave her a kiss on both cheeks. His intent was to show his knowledge of her culture. However, he—as a complete stranger—insulted and embarrassed this woman by kissing her.

It is important to understand kisses—how, when, where and to whom they are given. They may not be real kisses at all. Women may appear to be kissing cheeks when greeting someone, when actually they are brushing cheeks and "kissing the air."

The number of times people kiss is different.

Also, the *number* of times people kiss is different. Some countries kiss once, some twice, and some once for a business associate and twice for a personal friend. Know the kissing rules for the countries you will be visiting. See the "Meeting and Greeting" section of each chapter.

When you've traveled hundreds of miles to develop a new business relationship, you need to make the best impression in those critical first minutes. Your chances of creating a good impression improve enormously if you've done your homework. Knowing what initial behaviors you are likely to encounter allows you to relax and project a positive image.

You need to make the best impression in those critical first minutes.

Put Your Best Foot Forward

9.
NAMES AND TITLES

There is no sweeter sound to anyone's ear than the sound of his or her own name, used often and pronounced correctly. North Americans tend to be very casual when it comes to names—we may even laugh when we slaughter names of more than one syllable.

The United States is definitely a "first name" country. We shift from surnames to first names almost as soon as we meet each other. We consider it warm, comfortable and friendly to do so. We seldom use titles for anyone except medical doctors. Indeed, we view the use of titles as phony.

North Americans have plenty of status symbols. Among other things, we judge each other by where we went to school, how big our houses are and what kinds of cars we drive.

For South Americans, names and titles are status symbols. They speak to a person's family history, education, profession and position in a

Faux Pas

Incorrect use of titles is an insult.

company, community and perhaps even his or her country. People are put on a pedestal if they carry an important name or title. Understanding and respecting this tradition is essential to making friends and doing business in South America. Correct use of a person's name and title shows honor to the person.

For North Americans who have been reared with a "Just call me Bill" approach, the concern much of the world has about names and titles seems superficial. If this is your attitude, change it. In South America, misuse of someone's name and/or title can cause problems ranging from making a colleague uncomfortable to creating an international incident.

Keep in mind, however, that name usage is changing rapidly in South America. Today, young people and people who have worked, studied or traveled a great deal, especially in North America, may immediately call you by your first name and introduce themselves to you using their first names.

Correct use of names and titles is one of the most complicated and difficult things for an international traveler in South America. While there were specific rules in the past, today the name game is in flux due to changing economic, social and political situations. However, the following rules are a good starting point.

GENERAL RULES FOR NAMES AND TITLES

- Do your homework. Know the correct rules of name usage in each country.

- Do not use first names until invited to do so or until the other person repeatedly uses your first name.

- Ask each person what name they prefer to be called.

- Ask for a business card so you can see the correct spelling and correct title.

- Listen to pronunciation when introduced. Ask for a name to be repeated if you didn't hear it correctly. As soon as possible, jot down the phonetic pronunciation of a name.

- Help the person introducing you with your name.

- Say your name slowly and pronounce it clearly.

- Many women, especially those in business, government and the professions, have chosen to keep their own name rather than take their husbands'. Do not assume that a woman has the same surname as her husband.

Faux Pas

Do not use first names until invited to do so.

- Finally, in this matter as in all others, remember that every country has its own distinct differences. In Paraguay, for example, almost everyone has two first names as well as two last names.

NAMES

IN ALL COUNTRIES EXCEPT BRAZIL

- Most South Americans use two surnames. The given name is first, father's surname second, and mother's surname last. Generally a person is addressed in conversation by his or her father's surname.

  Example: Juan Valdez Sánchez would most likely be introduced and addressed as Señor Juan Valdez or Señor Valdez. Juan's father was Señor Valdez, his mother Señora Sánchez.

- When a woman marries, if she chooses to take her husband's name she appends it to her name by adding "de (husband's surname)" to her name. A woman is then addressed by her husband's surname. Many married South American women are choosing not to take their husbands' surnames. In this case, they continue to be addressed by their fathers' surnames.

  Example: Estela Medina Coscia de Valdez is introduced and addressed in

conversation as Señora Estela Valdez or Señora Valdez. Estela is married to Señor Valdez and has taken his name. If, however, Estela chose not to take her husband's name, the "de Valdez" would be omitted and she would be addressed as Señora Medina.

- A person's full name is used in written letters, legal documents, etc.

IN BRAZIL

- In Brazil, a person's given name is followed by the mother's surname, then the father's surname. Generally in conversation a person is addressed by his/her father's surname.

  Example: Pedro Álvares Cabral is addressed in conversation as Senhor Cabral. Pedro's mother was Senhora Álvares and his father was Senhor Cabral.

TITLES

Most people should be addressed by their title and surname.

Most people should be addressed by their title and surname. Only children, family members and close friends address each other by their given names.

Anyone who has graduated from college or holds a position in business or government should be addressed as "Doctor(a)" unless they specifically ask you to do otherwise.

TITLES IN SPANISH-SPEAKING COUNTRIES

English	Spanish	Pronunciation
Mr.	Señor	sen-YOHR
Mrs.	Señora	sen-YOHR-ah
Miss (unmarried women)	Señorita	sen-yohr-EET-ah
Respectful title (Sir/Madam)	Don/Doña	dohn(yah)
Doctor	Doctor(a)	doc-TOR(ah)
Teacher/Professor	Profesor(a)	pro-fay-SOR(ah)
Engineer	Ingeniero/a	een-HEN-e-air-oh/ah
Architect	Arquitecto/a	ar-kee-TEC-to/ah
Lawyer	Abogado/a	ah-bo-GAH-doh/dah

Don and Doña are used with a person's first name in some countries to show friendship and respect. They are generally used with older people with whom one is familiar: grandparents of close friends, an old neighbor, highly respected older colleagues, etc. Do not use this title for a new acquaintance, or for anyone you have not known for a long time. A person never refers to himself or herself by Don/Doña.

Examples:

Juan Valdez Sánchez –   Don Juan

Estela Medina Coscia – Doña Estela

TITLES IN BRAZIL

English	Portuguese	Pronunciation
Mr.	Senhor	seen-YOHR
Mrs.	Senhora	seen-YOHR-ah
Miss (unmarried women)	Senhorita	seen-yohr-EE-tah
Doctor	Doutor(a)	do-TOHR (ah)
Professor	Professor/a	pro-fess-OHR (ah)
Engineer	Engenheiro/a	en-zhen-AIR-oh (ah)
Architect	Arquitecto/a	ar-kee-TEK-to (ah)
Lawyer	Advogado/a	ad-vo-GAH-do (ah)

- O Senhor/A Senhora (to give deference) are often used.

Correct name use is challenging. However, it is worth the effort. It shows consideration for your host or guest, and will make you more comfortable once you've learned the correct usage.

Put Your Best Foot Forward

10.
LANGUAGE

To learn another's language is the greatest of compliments. The warmth, appreciation and welcome you will receive is incomparable. Nothing bespeaks your interest and concern more than taking the time to learn someone's language.

However, most North Americans are not multi-lingual and don't have the time to become so as adults. We are very lucky, however, because English is the business language of the world and is becoming the second language of choice worldwide. In South America, many schools require it through secondary school. There is a good chance that your South American colleagues will speak at least some English.

There is a good chance that your South American colleagues will speak at least some English.

When someone whose native language is not English is speaking English for your benefit, keep in mind the years of study it took for him or her to be able to do so. It is important to show your appreciation by being a considerate listener and speaker.

LISTENING

- Listen carefully for the gist of what is being said. Try not to ask your colleague to repeat.

- Never correct anyone's pronunciation, "fill in the blank" during pauses or finish a sentence for someone.

- Never act bored or impatient.

- Always follow up with a written fax, letter or e-mail stating what was discussed.

- Always assume an error in communication has occurred if someone has said or written something you consider insulting. Ask for clarification.

THANK YOU MR. AMBASSADOR

I sat next to a young diplomat one evening at a dinner party in Vienna. Very proud of his new international skills and position, he tried to test his charm on me. In a very flattering manner, he leaned toward me and said, "Mrs. Bosrock, what I like best about you are your blue eyes and your big mouth."

Somehow, "thank you" didn't seem like an appropriate response. Fortunately, an older and more seasoned gentleman sitting at my right came to my rescue. He said, "Mrs. Bosrock, I believe my colleague means that he admires your blue eyes and your 'full lips.'" Thank you, Mr. Ambassador.

- Apologize for not being able to speak your hosts' or guests' language and thank them for speaking English.

- Speak a little slower than your normal pace, using shorter sentences and simpler words. Do not, however, give the impression that you are speaking to children.

- Learn a few simple, polite phrases in your hosts' language—enough to show you are trying.

- Learn how to greet and thank your hosts, and learn a short toast. It doesn't have to be perfect. Your efforts will be greatly appreciated.

- Avoid using sports terms, idioms, slang and colloquialisms: "We're batting a thousand," "We've got you covered," etc.

Rule of Thumb

Learn a few simple, polite phrases in your hosts' language.

GET MY DRIFT?

Larry King, one of North America's best and most popular talk show hosts, interviewed Yasar Arafat in March 1997. Mr. Arafat speaks seven languages fluently. However, when Larry King asked "Is he a big player?", "How do you like him 'as a guy'?" and "Did he give you your due?", Mr. Arafat looked puzzled and confused. I'm sure he wondered if English was one of the languages he knew!

SPANISH PHRASES

English	Spanish	Pronunciation
Good morning/day	Buenos días	bway-nohs DEE-ahs
Good afternoon	Buenas tardes (until 8 p.m.)	bway-nahs TAHR-dehs
Good evening	Buenas noches (after dark)	bway-nahs NOH-chehs
Pleased to meet you	Encantado (said by man)	en-ken-TAH-doe
	Encantada (said by woman)	en-ken-TAH-dah
How are you?	¿Cómo está usted?	KOH-moh ehs-TAH oos-TEHD
Hello (informal)	Hola	OH-la
Yes	Sí	See
No	No	Noh
Please	Por favor	pohr fah-VOHR
Thank you	Gracias	GRAH-see-ahs
You're welcome	De nada	day NAH-dah
Excuse me	Perdóneme	perh-DOHN-nay-may
Good-bye	Adiós	as-DYOHS
Good bye/See you later (informal)	Hasta luego	AH-sta loo-AY-go
"To your health"—a toast. Also said after someone sneezes.	Salud	sah-LOOD

PORTUGUESE PHRASES

English	Portuguese	Pronunciation
Good morning/day	Bom dia	bong DEE-uh
Good afternoon	Boa tarde	BOH-uh tard
Good evening	Boa noite	BOH-uh noyt
Pleased to meet you	Muito prazer	MUY-tu pra-ZERR
How are you?	Como está?	KOH-moo shta
Yes	Sim	seeng
No	Não	NAH-oo
Please	Por favor	por fa-VOR
Thank you (by man)	Obrigado	o-bree-GAH-doo
Thank you (by woman)	Obrigada	o-bree-GAH-duh
You're welcome	De nada	day NAH-dah
Excuse me	Com licença	com lee-SEN-sa
Good-bye	Adeus	a-DAY-oosh
"To your health"—a toast	Á sua Saúde	a sua sa-OOD

It is important to remember that each country has a slightly different dialect spiced with local idioms and perhaps influenced by other languages. You may speak Spanish or Portuguese and still not understand all that is being said. If you hire an interpreter, make sure he or she speaks the local dialect. It is particularly nice to learn a few local terms or expressions special to the particular region or country you are visiting.

It is particularly nice to learn a few local terms or expressions.

In several South American countries, the Spanish spoken is the dialect of Castile, Spain.

People from those countries will say *"Yo hablo castellano"* instead of *"Yo hablo español"* for "I speak Spanish."

Remember, trying counts and mistakes made while trying are "good" mistakes. When you speak at least a few words of another's language, you show interest in people and their country. The effort and the positive attitude toward the people of the country will be greatly appreciated.

LONG LIVE THE POTATO

David, a North American friend of mine, tells the story of one attempt to speak Spanish in Mexico.

A devout Catholic, David drove south from Minnesota to celebrate the papal visit to Mexico. Overcome with emotion upon seeing His Holiness, David ran through the streets of Mexico City shouting "¡Viva la papa! ¡Viva la papa!" David's newfound Mexican friend, while sharing his excitement, thought it prudent to correct David's Spanish a little. "The Spanish word for 'pope' is 'el papa,'" the Mexican explained. "You're shouting 'Long live the potato.'"

SMALL TALK

We always worry about not being able to speak the language when we visit another country. The truth is, you'll be judged more by your conversational ability than your language ability. Bringing up a taboo topic will at the very least make your hosts uncomfortable and at worst insult and offend them. At the same time, there are certain things people enjoy discussing and will genuinely appreciate your inquiring about.

Before you visit any country, I suggest you check the news from that country for a few weeks. You will learn many interesting and important current facts, as well as some handy conversation starters.

Fortunately, finding international news is easier than ever today, thanks to on-line services and the Internet. I used my on-line service extensively while writing this book. Every day or two I did a search for news articles having to do with South America and South American countries. When I was talking with South Americans for my research, they were delighted when I could discuss current events in their countries.

TIPS FOR CONVERSATION IN SOUTH AMERICA

DO

- Ask informed questions about the country: its history, art, music and culture.

- Talk about sports, especially local teams and heroes. Many South Americans are mad

Many South Americans are mad about sports.

about sports, especially soccer (almost everywhere!) and baseball (in Venezuela particularly).

- Ask questions about politics. Many South Americans consider politics a passion and will enjoy discussing it with you. But refrain from giving your opinion and making comparisons.

- Ask about your host's children.

- Ask to taste the wonderful coffee of the country you are visiting if it is a coffee-producing region. Remember that coffee has built several cities in South America. People in Venezuela, Colombia and Brazil will especially appreciate your interest.

- Be prepared to be interrupted frequently by someone wanting to share his or her point of view. In much of South America, this is not considered impolite, but rather signifies interest.

DO NOT

- Do not use the words "America" or "American."

- Do not give your opinion on the politics of the country you are visiting. In day-to-day life in the United States, it makes little difference whether the Democrats or Republicans are in power. This is not true in South America, where the differences between the parties are drastic and make a great difference in the course the countries take.

- Do not classify anyone by race or ethnic background. People in South America are Brazilians, Colombians, Peruvians, etc.— not white, black, mestizo, etc. You may meet people who identify themselves primarily with their ethnic group, but do not presume.

- Never criticize or compare any country with another, especially your own.

- Never discuss the drug problem in a light or flippant manner.

11.

BODY LANGUAGE

ACTIONS SPEAK LOUDER THAN WORDS

If each and every one of us spoke every language fluently, we would still make errors when communicating with people from different cultures. Researchers have determined that 85 percent of communication is non-verbal.

Our body language—eye contact, posture, how we sit, when we smile, where we put our hands and feet—all send positive and negative messages to other people. We misread these signals constantly within our own culture. Can you imagine the mixed signals we can send and receive when dealing with other cultures? Even if you are confident that you understand your South American counterparts' words perfectly, if you misinterpret their body language (or allow them to misinterpret yours) you may not be communicating as well as you think.

Researchers have determined that 85 percent of communication is non-verbal.

NO FOOL LIKE AN OLD FOOL

My brother, a portly gentleman in his mid-fifties, attended a legal conference in Miami recently. At one function, he happened to be seated next to a young, beautiful woman from a South American country. When the conference ended, this lovely young woman said good-bye to my brother and kissed him once on each cheek.

My brother—a happily married man for thirty years—returned home very full of himself, convinced that this young lady had fallen deeply in love with him.

It broke my heart to tell him that this woman was not overwhelmed by his charm. This is the way most, if not all, women from South America would have said farewell to anyone they had spent some time with.

TOUCHING

There is not much "shade of gray" when it comes to touchers and non-touchers. People who like to touch *really like* touching and people who don't like to touch *really hate* being touched. If you are the latter, you may be somewhat uncomfortable with South Americans, who are, as a whole, very warm and "touchy."

Men embrace each other after an acquaintance is established. Women kiss each other's cheeks. Men kiss and embrace women friends. It is very important not to misunderstand this warm interaction. This has no sexual overtones—just the opposite. It is a sign of respect and friendship. For a South American gentleman not to kiss the cheek of a woman he knows would be extremely rude.

South Americans do *not* randomly grab people and hug them. Touching is a behavior reserved for friends and family members in almost all cultures. Touchers hug and kiss their children, spouses and close friends. They generally do not want to be touched by strangers, people they meet occasionally, new business associates or new acquaintances.

South Americans are very perceptive people.

When you become acquainted with people, they will be more comfortable with you if you reciprocate kisses and hugs. However, South Americans are very perceptive people. If you really can't bear touching, extend your hand to shake—wearing a big friendly smile—and they'll get the message.

A TOUCHING MATTER

A lovely woman from Norway told me about a difficulty she had while working in South America. She truly loved the people she worked with, but coming from a home and a country in which she never saw any body contact even between her parents, she was incredibly uncomfortable attending parties where everyone would kiss and hug "hello" and "good-bye"—and nearly everything in between. She finally explained her problem to her friends. They were very understanding, particularly since she had embraced so much else of their culture. During the remaining months of her stay in South America, she greeted friends by smiling warmly, and saying, "kiss, kiss, kiss."

PERSONAL SPACE

Personal space in South America is smaller than North Americans are used to. People tend to stand twelve to eighteen inches apart, opposed to the two to three feet common in the United States—a distance which South Americans may view as cold and unfriendly.

- Never step back when a person moves close to you.

- Don't show signs of discomfort, which would appear rude to your counterpart.

- Don't misread close personal space as a sexual advance.

Never step back when a person moves close to you.

TIPS ON BODY LANGUAGE
IN SOUTH AMERICA

- Smile! Your smiles will be appreciated and returned.

- Make and maintain direct eye contact. It is extremely impolite not to do so while conversing.

- South Americans often hold handshakes longer than North Americans, or accompany them with a squeeze of the arm or a hug.

- Men cross their legs at the knee. Crossing your legs at the ankle is viewed as feminine in some countries.

- Do not beckon anyone with your index finger.

- Cover your mouth when you yawn.

- Never mimic what you think is a national gesture.

- Your South American counterparts will likely be familiar with North American gestures. However, to avoid misunderstandings, keep your gestures to a minimum.

Never mimic what you think is a national gesture.

12.
TRADITION AND SUPERSTITION

Most of your South American colleagues will probably not be concerned with superstitions. Many of the educated and sophisticated South Americans you meet will scoff at the very idea that actions can draw luck, either good or bad.

But even while laughing at such ideas, many will follow the age-old practices. Be familiar with the following:

- Never put your purse on the floor or your money will run away.

- Never take shells or coral into your home or you'll have bad luck.

- Eat a tablespoon of lentils on New Year's Eve/Day to bring good luck in money, love and business.

- Sweeping someone's feet could cause one never to marry.

- Never put money or your hat on a bed.

- Never pass salt hand to hand.

- Tuesday the 13th is an unlucky day.

- Putting a broom by the door, with bristles facing upward, will ensure a visitor won't stay long.

Never laugh at someone's devotion to following such practices. We all have little rituals we follow for much the same reasons.

13.

DINING AND SOCIAL EVENTS

Food offered is friendship offered. When your hosts offer you a local delicacy or a national specialty, they are offering you a sample of their culture as well as their friendship. They are giving you the best they have and if you reject it, you are rejecting them, their culture and their friendship. This is not an auspicious way to begin a mutually beneficial relationship. The food in South America is very good and is generally not unusual for North Americans or Europeans.

Food offered is friendship offered.

A woman from South Dakota was visiting her fiancé's family in Argentina. The Argentines prepared a huge feast to welcome this young woman. The dinner consisted mostly of meat dishes and this woman was a vegetarian. Instead of quietly eating a little of what was served, she decided to make herself at home and went into the kitchen to prepare a salad. Needless to say, her future in-laws were hurt and insulted.

OUT GOES THE BRIDE

South Americans are warm and gracious hosts. If you are invited to a party, you will enjoy music, dancing and a lot of food and drink. Join in, eat the food offered, drink the drinks offered and try to dance, even if you aren't great. If you can merengue or salsa, you will be very popular!

DINING

South Americans serve elegantly, in the European style.

- Continental Style: The fork is held in the left hand, tines facing down. The knife is held in the right hand. The knife is used to cut and push food onto your fork.

- All silverware is arranged with the utensil to be used first laid on the outside, farthest from the plate. Forks are always placed to the left of the plate. Spoons and knives are always placed to the right of the plate. If a

The kids connection to living a fun-filled, drug-free lifestyle

Where positive peer pressure flourishes in the fight against teenage drug use

"Before D-FY-IT came to my school, there were drugs everywhere. Every day I was faced with someone wanting me to do drugs... on the school bus, in the bathrooms, even in the hallways, Now that D-FY-IT is here, the drug problem isn't so bad anymore... most of the kids in my school are D-FY-IT members cuz you're not cool if you're not in D-FY-IT. Now the gang members are D-FY-IT members too."

-11th grade student

"D-FY-IT is dedicated to improving our neighborhoods and our schools. It is truly an amazing and effective program. As a school principal, I am an eyewitness to the success of this wonderful program. The look on a child's face when they receive their D-FY-IT membership credentials or the proud feeling they experience while performing community service cannot be described."

-Dade County middle school principal

Would you believe that 4,198 teens in ten Dade County schools are drug-free and proud to prove it? D-FY-IT is a unique and innovative program: a community service club for drug-free kids in middle and senior high schools whose student members commit to active community service participation and volunteer to be randomly drug screened. D-FY-IT depends on donations from individuals,

businesses, corporations and foundations to enable the program to exist and expand to schools throughout the nation and the world. By supporting D-FY-IT, a giant step will be taken, in your honor, to keep kids off drugs and to ensure NOW that we are guaranteeing our responsible, productive community decision-makers of tomorrow.

If you would like information on D-FY-IT or how you can support this unprecedented youth movement, please contact:

D-FY-IT
(Drug-Free Youth in Town)

9990 SW 77th Avenue, PH-18,
Miami, Florida 33156

305-271-5444
Fax 305-271-5006

Pick up the phone.
Pick up the miles.

1-800-FLY-FREE

Now when you sign up with MCI® you can earn up to 8,000 bonus miles on any one of the airlines below.* Then earn another 5 miles for every dollar** (or 1 flight credit for every $150) you spend on MCI long distance, cellular, paging, or calls with your MCI Card® from anywhere in the world. You're going to use these services anyway. Why not rack up the miles while you're doing it?

Is this a great time, or what? :-) **MCI**

 NORTHWEST WORLDPERKS® *MIDWEST EXPRESS AIRLINES* HAWAIIAN GOLD·PLUS. ▲ **Delta Air Lines** **SkyMiles**® Continental *OnePass*

Pick Up The Phone Pick Up The Miles

Calling Card
123 456 7890 1234
J. D. SMITH
WaltDisney

You earn frequent flyer miles when you travel internationally – why not when you call internationally?

- Callers can earn frequent flyer miles with one of MCI's airline partners.

- Access to the U.S. from more than 125 countries and places around the world

- Operators who speak your language

- 24-hour customer service

Please call MCI for complete program details at 1-800-444-1616

Reference Guide for MCI Card Calling in the U.S. and Worldwide

Calling Card
123 456 7890 1234
J.D. SMITH

COUNTRY	WORLDPHONE TOLL-FREE ACCESS #
# American Samoa	633-2MCI (633-2624)
# Antigua (Available from public card phones only)	#2
◆ Argentina	0800-5-1002
✜ Aruba	800-888-8
# Australia (CC) ◆	1-800-551-111
To call using OPTUS ■	
To call using TELSTRA ■	1-800-881-100
◆ Austria (CC) ✜	022-903-012
# Bahamas (CC)	1-800-888-8000
Bahrain	800-002
Barbados	1-800-888-8000
Belarus	
From Brest, Vitebsk, Grodno, Minsk	8-800-103
From Gomel and Mogilev regions	8-10-800-103
# Belgium (CC) ✜	0800-10012
# Belize	
From Hotels	557
From Payphones	815
# Bermuda ✜	1-800-888-8000
◆ Bolivia ◆	0-800-2222
# Brazil (CC)	000-8012
# British Virgin Islands ✜	1-800-888-8000
# Brunei	800-011
Bulgaria	00800-0001
# Canada (CC)	1-800-888-8000
Cayman Islands	1-800-888-8000
# Chile (CC) ✜	800-207-300
To call using CTC ■	800-360-180
To call using ENTEL ■	
# China ✜ (Available from most major cities)	108-12
◆ Colombia (CC) ◆	980-16-0001
# Costa Rica ◆	0800-012-2222
# Cote D'Ivoire	1001
◆ Croatia (CC) ✜	99-385-0112
# Cyprus ◆	080-90000
# Czech Republic (CC) ✜	00-42-000112
# Denmark (CC) ✜	8001-0022
# Dominica	1-800-888-8000
Dominican Republic (CC)	1-800-888-8000
◆ Ecuador (CC)	999-170
# Egypt (CC) ✜ (Outside of Cairo, dial 02 first)	355-5770
El Salvador	800-1767
Federated States of Micronesia	624
# Fiji	004-890-1002
# Finland (CC) ✜	0800-102-80
◆ France (CC) ✜	0800-99-0019
# French Antilles (CC) (Martinique, Guadeloupe)	0800-99-0019
French Guiana (CC)	0-800-99-0019
◆ Gambia ◆	00-1-99
# Germany (CC)	0130-0012
◆ Greece (CC) ✜	00-800-1211
◆ Grenada ✜	1-800-888-8000

COUNTRY	WORLDPHONE TOLL-FREE ACCESS #
# Guam (CC)	950-1022
# Guatemala (CC) ✜	99-99-189
◆ Guyana	177
# Haiti (CC) ✜	193
Honduras ✜	122
# Hong Kong (CC)	800-1121
# Hungary (CC) ✜	00▼800-01411
# Iceland (CC) ◆	800-9002
# India (CC) ◆	000-127
# Indonesia (CC) ◆	001-801-11
Iran ✜ (SPECIAL PHONES ONLY)	
# Ireland (CC)	1-800-55-1001
# Israel (CC) ◆	177-150-2727
# Italy (CC) ✜	172-1022
Jamaica	1-800-888-8000
# Japan (CC) ✜	0039-121
To call using KDD ■	0066-55-121
To call using IDC ■	0044-11-121
To call using ITJ ■	
# Jordan	18-800-001
# Kazakhstan (CC)	8-800-131-4321
# Kenya (Available from most major cities)	080011
# Korea (CC) ✜	550-2255
Press red button, 03, then ✦	
Phone Booth✜	
Military Bases	
# Kuwait	800-MCI (800-624)
Lebanon ✜	600-MCI (600-624)
# Liechtenstein (CC) ✦	0800-89-0222
Luxembourg	0800-0112
# Macao	0800-131
# Malaysia (CC) ◆	1-800-80-0012
# Malta	0800-89-0120
Marshall Islands	1-800-888-8000
# Mexico ▲	95-800-674-7000
# Monaco (CC) ✜	800-90-019
Morocco	00-211-0012
# Netherlands (CC) ✜	0800-022-9122
# Netherlands Antilles (CC) ✜	001-800-950-1022
# New Zealand (CC)	000-912
Nicaragua (CC) (Outside of Managua, dial 02 first)	166
◆ Norway (CC) ✜	800-19912
# Panama	108
Military Bases	2810-108
# Papua New Guinea ✜	05-07-19140
◆ Paraguay ✜	008-11-800
# Peru	0800-500-10
◆ Philippines (CC) ✜	105-14
To call using PLDT ◆	105-14
To call using PHILCOM ■	1026-14

COUNTRY	WORLDPHONE TOLL-FREE ACCESS #
◆ Poland (CC) ✜	00-800-111-21-22
# Portugal (CC) ✜	05-017-1234
# Puerto Rico (CC)	1-800-888-8000
◆ Qatar ★	0800-012-77
# Romania (CC) ✜	01-800-1800
◆ Russia (CC) ✜ ❖	
To call using ROSTELCOM ■	747-3322
To call using SOVINTEL ■	960-2222
# Saipan (CC) ✜ ◆	950-1022
# San Marino (CC) ✜	172-1022
◆ Saudi Arabia (CC)	1-800-11
# Singapore	8000-112-112
# Slovak Republic (CC)	00421-00112
# Slovenia	080-8808
# South Africa (CC)	0800-99-0011
◆ Spain (CC) ✜	900-99-0014
# Sri Lanka (Outside of Colombo, dial 01 first)	440100
# St. Lucia ✜	0039-121
# St. Vincent (CC)	0066-55-121
# Sweden (CC) ✜	020-795-922
# Switzerland (CC) ✜	0800-89-0222
# Syria	0080-1
# Taiwan (CC) ✜	0080-13-4567
# Thailand ✦	001-999-1-2001
# Trinidad & Tobago ✜	1-800-888-8001
# Turkey (CC) ✜ ◆	00-8001-1177
# Turks and Caicos ✜	1-800-888-8000
# Ukraine (CC) ✜	8▼10-013
# United Arab Emirates ✦	800-111
# United Kingdom (CC)	
To call using BT ■	0800-89-0222
To call using MERCURY ■	0500-89-0222
# United States (CC)	1-800-888-8000
# Uruguay	000-412
# U.S. Virgin Islands (CC)	1-800-888-8000
# Vatican City (CC) ✜	172-1022
◆ Venezuela (CC) ✜ ◆	800-1114-0
# Vietnam	1201-1022

Automation available from most locations.

(CC) Country-to-country calling available to/from most international locations.

✜ Limited availability.

◆ Wait for second dial tone.

▲ When calling from public phones, use phones marked LADATEL.

★ International communications carrier.

✦ Not available from public pay phones.

❖ Regulation does not permit intra-Japan calls.

▼ Public phones may require deposit of coin or phone card for dial tone.

● Local service fee in U.S. currency required to complete call.

The MCI Card® with WorldPhone® Service...
The easy way to call when traveling worldwide.

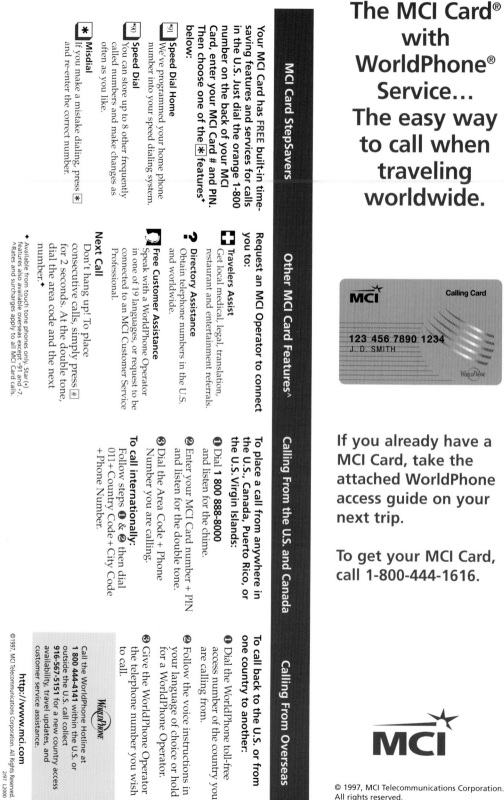

Calling Card

123 456 7890 1234
J. D. SMITH

WorldPhone

If you already have a MCI Card, take the attached WorldPhone access guide on your next trip.

To get your MCI Card, call 1-800-444-1616.

MCI Card StepSavers

Your MCI Card has FREE built-in time-saving features and services for calls in the U.S. Just dial the orange 1-800 number on the back of your MCI Card, enter your MCI Card # and PIN. Then choose one of the ✳ features♦ below:

✳1 Speed Dial Home
We've programmed your home phone number into your speed dialing system.

✳0 Speed Dial
You can store up to 8 other frequently called numbers and make changes as often as you like.

✳ Misdial
If you make a mistake dialing, press ✳ and re-enter the correct number.

Other MCI Card Features^

Request an MCI Operator to connect you to:

➕ Travelers Assist
Get local medical, legal, translation, restaurant and entertainment referrals.

❓ Directory Assistance
Obtain telephone numbers in the U.S. and worldwide.

📞 Free Customer Assistance
Speak with a WorldPhone Operator in one of 19 languages, or request to be connected to an MCI Customer Service Professional.

Next Call
Don't hang up! To place consecutive calls, simply press # for 2 seconds. At the double tone, dial the area code and the next number.

♦ Available from touch tone phones only. Star(✳) features also available overseas except ✳91 and ✳7.
^ Rates and surcharges apply to all MCI Card calls.

Calling From the U.S. and Canada

To place a call from anywhere in the U.S., Canada, Puerto Rico, or the U.S. Virgin Islands:

❶ Dial **1 800 888-8000** and listen for the chime.

❷ Enter your MCI Card number + PIN and listen for the double tone.

❸ Dial the Area Code + Phone Number you are calling.

To call internationally:
Follow steps ❶ & ❷ then dial 011+ Country Code + City Code + Phone Number.

Calling From Overseas

To call back to the U.S. or from one country to another:

❶ Dial the WorldPhone toll-free access number of the country you are calling from.

❷ Follow the voice instructions in your language of choice or hold for a WorldPhone Operator.

❸ Give the WorldPhone Operator the telephone number you wish to call.

Call the WorldPhone Hotline at **1 800 444-4141** within the U.S. or outside the U.S. call collect **916-567-5151** for a new country access availability, travel updates, and customer service assistance.

http://www.mci.com

WorldPhone

MCI

fork is placed to the right of the spoons, it is a cocktail fork. The butter knife is laid on the butter plate. Dessert silverware is brought on as dessert is served or, in some countries, laid at the top of the plate.

- If your knife and fork are in any way open on your plate, it means that you would like more food or that you are not finished eating.

- When finished eating, place your knife and fork side by side on the plate in the 5:25 position.

- The head and foot of the table are generally reserved for the host and hostess or the mother and father. The guests of honor are seated to the right of the host and hostess. Wait for your host to designate your seat at the table and invite you to be seated.

Offer food or drink to others before helping yourself.

- Never begin eating until everyone is served and your hostess has begun. Offer food or drink to others before helping yourself. Taste everything that is served.

- Your napkin should be on your lap at all times during the meal.

- Never lick your fingers.

- Rest your hands and wrists on the table, never in your lap. Never put your elbows on the table. Never touch food with your hands.

- Never smoke at the table without asking permission of your host and other guests.

- Do not speak with food in your mouth. Never make strange noises with your mouth (smacking). Never burp, which is very crass.

RESTAURANTS

- When guests are invited to a restaurant, the host pays for the meal. What we in North America call "going Dutch" (splitting the bill), South Americans call "doing as the North Americans."

- Raise your hand or index finger to signal a waiter.

- Water is generally not served with the meal. If you would like water, ask for it.

- Your bill will not be presented until you request it.

THE ART OF NOT EATING — POLITELY

If you have a weak stomach or really dislike the food served by your hosts, here are some helpful hints.

- Never ask what a dish is until you have finished eating.

- Take a big gulp of the pink stuff (Pepto-Bismol) before you go to dinner.

- Cut food into small bites. Don't chew particularly unpleasant food, just swallow fast. Sometimes the consistency is worse than the taste.

- Taste everything, and try to eat at least a little of it. If you really cannot eat something, a taste is polite. When offered seconds of something you don't like, say "Thank you, but please allow me to finish this portion first." Eat slower and talk more.

- Never make a negative comment, joke or a face about what is served.

- Engage in ongoing conversation with your dinner partners. It will get your mind off the food and take up time until the next course is served.

Never make a negative comment, joke or a face about what is served.

TOASTING

- If possible, make a toast in your hosts' or guests' language. Even if it isn't perfect, it will be enjoyed and appreciated.

- Make your toast short. Toasts are commonly done to health and happiness. An accompanying story (in English, unless your Spanish or Portuguese is excellent) will be appreciated. Don't tell jokes— they seldom cross cultural lines.

- It is acceptable for women to give toasts.

- The guest of honor will probably be toasted and should reciprocate by giving a toast of thanks.

- The typical toast in the Spanish speaking countries is "*salud*" (sah-LOOD), meaning "To your health" or "Cheers."

- A typical toast in Portuguese is *á sua saúde* (a sua sa-OOD), used formally and informally.

ENTERTAINING SOUTH AMERICANS

There is no place like home. Your city's best restaurants cannot compare to an invitation to your house. Visitors always enjoy seeing how you live, how you decorate your home, what art and music you like and especially meeting your family. An invitation to your home is a special event not soon forgotten by your guests.

Some points to remember when entertaining South Americans:

- Check for dietary restrictions.

- Serve good quality and very strong coffee. South Americans refer disparagingly to the "brown water" North Americans often serve.

Serve good quality and very strong coffee.

- Never send an invitation with the time the function will end.

- Never expect a South American to arrive on time for a party or dinner. Allow for one-half to one hour (or more) late arrivals.

- South Americans, especially Argentines, like barbecued meats. This does not mean meat slathered with barbecue sauce. If you like barbecue sauce, serve it on the side.

GENERAL RULES FOR
DINING AND ENTERTAINMENT

- Never arrive at the designated time for a party. Always arrive at least one-half to one hour late. South American guests may arrive as much as two hours late. A VIP may arrive even later.

- Don't go to a party hungry. An 8:00 party may not serve food until 9:30 and dinner may not begin until 11:00.

- Arrive with flowers or chocolates for the hostess.

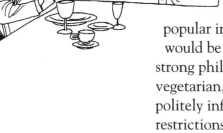

- Dinners are considered social events and are times to enjoy. Conversation is lively. Do not discuss business unless your host initiates it.

- Be prepared to eat meat. A vegetarian will be about as popular in South America as he or she would be in Texas. If you have medical or strong philosophical reasons for being a vegetarian, you may want to privately and politely inform your hosts of your restrictions before the event.

- Never finish dinner and leave. You should stay at least one-and-a-half hours after dessert to be polite. Dinner may last several hours. South Americans may dance and party until morning.

- There is normally a great deal of food and drink served at a party. People enjoy both but do not generally abuse either.

- There is always music and dancing at a South American party.

- Compliment the hostess on the meal.

- Always write a thank-you note promptly.

- Birthdays are a big, big deal! Even for first birthdays, parents hire caterers and musicians. A girl's fifteenth birthday, *cumpleaños de quince*, is an especially big celebration.

MENU TERMS

English	Portuguese	Spanish
Appetizers	Appertivos, Entradas	Aperitivos, Entradas
Main course	Menu	Plato principal, Plato fuerte
Dessert	Sobremesa	Postre
Bread	Páo	Pan
Soup	Sopa	Sopa
Vegetables	Vegetal	Verduras
Beef	Vaca	Carne de res
Chicken	Frango	Pollo
Pork	Porco	Cerdo
Lamb	Cordeiro	Cordero
Fish	Peixe	Pescado
Egg	Ovo	Huevo

14.
DRESS AND APPEARANCE

"Clothes make the man." However, in South America, clothes can also unmake the man or woman. Men as well as women are fashion-conscious and dress very well.

If you are visiting South America, take time to work on your appearance. South Americans make judgments based on appearance and clothing. Your dress is an indicator of your personality, social status and level of success in the business world. This is not the time to be humble or practical. Do not be ostentatious, but a flair is appreciated.

Men as well as women are fashion-conscious and dress very well.

GENERAL RULES

- Good grooming is vital! People will notice your hair and nails. Make sure your nails are clean and manicured.

- Do not underdress. If in doubt about what to wear for a particular occasion, err on the side of formality. Better yet, ask a knowledgeable colleague.

- Convey the look of personal substance.

- South Americans like and wear name brands.

- Wear good quality, well-polished shoes. Shoes are the first thing people notice. Never wear socks with sandals. South Americans find this extremely funny.

- Avoid wearing polyester and other synthetic fabrics; stick with cotton and lightweight wool.

- Remember that North American casual is quite different from South American casual, which is "smart casual." "Informal" in South America does not mean shorts and a T-shirt. Never wear shorts, T-shirts or tennis shoes unless you are absolutely certain they are appropriate for the occasion—and such occasions will be very rare. Never wear sloppy, dirty clothes.

- Jeans are worn by almost everyone, everywhere for casual dress—but only high style, fashionable jeans.

Never wear socks with sandals.

- Never go native—or what you think is native. There is nothing that looks sillier than someone trying to look like a local and not succeeding.

South American women are beautiful and work hard at looking great. They are aware of their appearance and their bodies. Whether a woman is an executive, government official or the spouse of an executive, she will be fashion-conscious. South American women want to "turn heads." They usually dress in a feminine—even sexy—manner without any problem.

WOMEN

- Dress for women in business will be professional with pizzazz—for example, shorter skirt lengths are common.

- Dress fashionably and not too conservatively, with a bit of flair. Look like a competent, knowledgeable and skilled person—but not like a man.

- A dress or skirt is always appropriate for a woman.

- The "little black dress" is always appropriate evening attire for women attending a dinner, the opera, the theater or a concert.

- For many "casual" occasions, silk blouses and long skirts are appropriate.

- South American women, especially older women, do not wear pants as often as North American women. Younger South Americans are changing this, however, and a dressy pair of pants is usually acceptable.

South American women want to "turn heads."

MEN

- Men dress elegantly and fashionably, but not "way out." Take navy, dark gray, black or pinstriped suits, light colored or white dress shirts, and good silk ties. These will be correct for any business meeting or evening event.

- Leave home light colored suits, sports coats and pants, plaid pants and shirts.

- Tropical weight wool is best for warm climates.

- South American men wear longer trousers than men in the U.S. Wear long dark socks as well—no ankles or legs showing, please!

- For "casual" or "informal" occasions, South American men may appear in linen blazers, pleated pants and good quality cotton shirts.

There is no worse feeling than "sticking out" because we feel we don't look good or appropriate for the occasion. If you happen to find yourself in this situation, never apologize; relax, make a mental note for future reference, and conduct yourself with dignity and good taste. Your personality will overcome any temporary deficiency in dress.

I attended a conference in Miami, Florida, hosted by a North American company and held for its South American affiliates. The conference chairperson invited everyone to attend the Friday meeting in casual attire.

On Friday morning, all the South American men arrived in designer shirts, pleated pants and Italian loafers. Most wore fashionable sport coats as well. The South American women were in long, lovely skirts and beautiful silk blouses. As the meeting began, one of the North American managers arrived wearing tennis shoes, shorts, a college sweatshirt and a baseball cap.

Not a word was spoken, but it was difficult to assess who was most uncomfortable at that meeting.

15.
PUNCTUALITY AND PACE

One of the greatest challenges you'll face in doing business in South America is understanding and accepting the local norms of punctuality and pace. It's important to understand that differences in such matters aren't necessarily good or bad—just different.

PUNCTUALITY

Many North Americans, Europeans and Asians view someone being late as showing a lack of respect and having sloppy, undisciplined personal habits—even being potentially unreliable as a partner or supplier.

Being "on time" is very different in South America. What's late in North America may well be early in South America. Lateness isn't considered rude or disrespectful. If you become angry or upset with your South American colleagues because they are late for an appointment, they probably won't expect or understand your anger and they will not feel guilty or apologize.

Lateness isn't considered rude or disrespectful.

7:00 P.M.
COCKTAILS
"BITTE"

The general manager of a German bank graciously offered to host a cocktail party for the South American delegation to the Bank of International Development annual meeting in Hamburg. The engraved invitation read, "7:00 p.m.— cocktails."

The German banker and his wife dressed elegantly and were at the door to greet guests at 6:30. At 8:45, not a single guest had arrived. The general manager was in a rage and asked his staff, "What kind of people did we invite to this party?" The answer: South Americans.

Remember that first obligations are to family and friends. A request from or discussion with a friend or family member *always* takes precedence over business. Meetings may not begin on time. However, most businesspeople who have dealt extensively in the international arena will make an attempt to be on time for business meetings.

Follow the guidelines in the country chapters regarding specific attitudes toward punctuality in those countries. If uncertain, ask! Ask your host, a friend or the concierge at your hotel. Keep in mind that in business it is better to err on the side of punctuality. For social events, it is better to be late.

PACE

Differences in pace are more difficult to understand and adjust to than differences in the sense of time. Pace deals with a sense of urgency (or lack of it) with making decisions, keeping promises, meeting deadlines—"getting the job done." Differences in pace have their roots in deeply ingrained habits and attitudes— in culture itself. The local pace seems natural and right to the person performing the task. This is where knowledge and patience are vital to the success of your project and your sanity.

The local pace seems natural and right to the person performing the task.

In North America, people believe "Where there's a will, there's a way." In South America, people believe that life follows a pre-ordained course in which human fate is determined by the will of God. This can cause a great deal of frustration and misunderstanding if you come from a society where "get it done yesterday" is on time.

WHO'S CRAZY?

A South American friend told me about meeting a North American consultant after work for a drink. In a most frustrated manner, the North American said, "This place drives me crazy. The pace of getting anything done is ridiculously slow." My friend asked me, "Didn't it ever enter his mind that he was in my country, and that we do business at a pace we enjoy? Maybe—just maybe—the North American pace is too fast!"

When a South American says "I'll phone you this afternoon" or "you'll get that report tomorrow," you may not get that call until the next day or the report until next week. This is not viewed as a lie or as incompetent behavior. South Americans know and understand this and you'll need to deal with it if you hope to survive in South America.

16.

STRICTLY BUSINESS

Unfortunately, most North Americans have not paid much attention to or taken time to learn about our neighbors to the South. The United States and the world cannot afford to ignore a continent that is called home by one-fifth of the world's population and is an incredibly rich source of natural resources.

Political stability has settled across the continent. Every country in South America is now a democracy. Stereotypes about unreliable governments are now simply untrue.

Most South American economies are doing better than they have in decades. Companies from the United States, Europe and Asia are rapidly expanding their operations in South America.

While the economic gap between the rich and poor remains large, there is also a growing middle class of professional people,

WHY SOUTH AMERICA?

Bill Gates can do what Madeleine Albright often can't.

No South American market is risk-free.

businesspeople, government employees and skilled workers.

No South American market is risk-free. The path to success will not be quick or without setbacks. But the possibilities are intriguing:

- In 1997, South America is expected to reach its fastest GDP growth since 1992. Latin American stocks rose by 15 percent in 1996, compared with 3.5 percent in Asia. (Source: International Finance Corporation emerging market index and Deutsche Morgan Grenfell.)

- Brazil, with 161 million people, has the second largest market in the Western Hemisphere, exceeded only by the United States.

- U.S. exports to Brazil have grown by 40 percent since 1994, to $11.4 billion in 1995. Annual direct investment rose by 370 percent since 1991. U.S. investments in Brazilian stock markets have grown from $760 million in 1991 to $22.6 billion in 1995. Brazil's sheer size and its rapidly growing middle class continue to attract foreign investment.

In 1997, South America is expected to reach its fastest GDP growth since 1992.

- Korea's Hyundai Group will invest US$3.38 billion in exploring natural resources and participating in infrastructure projects in

Brazil, Peru and Chile. "Latin America is a new frontier for us," South Korean President Kim Young-sam said after a "sales diplomacy" mission in September 1996.

- General Motors plans to invest $3.5 billion in factories in Brazil between now and the year 2000. Ford will contribute another $2.5 billion and Chrysler about $315 million. Volkswagen has invested $250 million in a high-profile, state-of-the-art facility.

- International banks are scrambling to get in on the "banking revolution" in Argentina. In September 1996, a record high US$14.1 billion was invested in foreign capital to Argentine assets.

- Growth in mineral investment is exploding. Venezuela alone may have the potential to increase gold production by a factor of thirteen over the next ten years.

Growth in mineral investment is exploding.

- A pharmaceutical revolution is poised to take place. South American countries are negotiating with international drug companies to jointly explore the enormous potential that awaits humanity from the medicinal uses of tropical plants.

- Japanese Prime Minister Ryutaro Hashimoto, on a tour that included Peru, Chile and Brazil, said, "The countries of

Latin America hold the key to the world's development in the 21st century."

Resources—human and natural—are abundant and have only begun to be explored. United States businesspeople who go to South America as partners—not exploiters—have wonderful opportunities and experiences awaiting them.

TREATIES

Trade, political, and economic cooperation throughout the Americas is steadily increasing. The threat of political instability and protectionism returning to this region has been greatly diminished.

FTAA - FREE TRADE AREA OF THE AMERICAS

34 Western Hemisphere countries (all except Cuba) met in May 1997 in Brazil to discuss building on the FTAA and reforms of economies which already have ended tariffs, quotas, government monopolies and currency restrictions.

NAFTA - NORTH AMERICAN FREE TRADE AGREEMENT

With White House support, Chile will soon attempt to enter NAFTA with Canada, Mexico and the United States.

MERCOSUR - THE SOUTHERN CONE MARKET

In an agreement similar to NAFTA, Argentina, Brazil, Paraguay and Uruguay entered into a treaty called Mercosur effective January 1, 1995. Mercosur creates a free trade zone that is an attempt to abolish all tariffs. It is possible for citizens of each member nation to travel to other nations of the treaty without a passport. Chile has elected to become an associate member. Mercosur countries will soon reach free trade agreements with Bolivia and Venezuela.

BUSINESS CARDS

- Business cards are commonly exchanged after initial introductions. There is no particular protocol for this procedure in South America.

- Print your cards in English on one side, Spanish or Portuguese on the other. While this is not absolutely necessary, it is a nice gesture. It shows you are in for the long haul, not just a quick buck.

RELATIONSHIPS

Personal relationships are the key to successful business in South America, where people are more important than laws, regulations or institutions.

CORPORATE CULTURE

Personal relationships are the key to successful business in South America.

Business relationships begin and develop as personal relationships. Who you are and whom you know are vital to your success in South America. You may have the best product at a very competitive price, but if you think you can blow into a country on Monday, do your business, sign a contract and be back home by the weekend, forget going to South America.

Connections are the way things get done in South America. People are used to dealing with people of their own class; when possible, they do business with relatives and friends. Nepotism is as natural as breathing.

Connections are the way things get done in South America.

ALL IN THE FAMILY

A North American manager asked his South American secretary to place a help-wanted ad in the local paper and the company newsletter for an open position. The secretary immediately phoned her unemployed nephew and told him to apply for the job. A week later, her boss, very upset that his instructions had not been followed, asked why she hadn't placed the ad. She replied, "I told my nephew and he applied. He is perfect for the job." The South American couldn't imagine posting a job for strangers when she had a relative who could fill it.

Employer/employee relationships are close and personal. Companies look after employees as a family would. Each is responsible for the other's well being and both expect loyalty.

STRUCTURE

In some South American countries, government is very active in directing and controlling the economy. Certain sectors of the economy may be under state control; however, privatization and liberalization are gradually and steadily underway.

Generally speaking, in South America, power and authority rest with a person—as compared with the United States, where power and authority rest with a job title. For the most part, decisions are centralized. The nature and type of decisions made are strongly influenced by the personality of the decision-maker.

The person in authority has the power to make decisions, period! He or she does not need to consult others. To question this authority would simply show a lack of confidence in the boss's judgment. Lower status persons do not put forward ideas that conflict with leaders.

The chain of command is respected in South America. This may take more time and be viewed as inefficient if you come from a society like the United States where "time is money."

THE SECRETARY

The first person you will probably talk to and meet with in South America is the secretary. Secretaries are very important people, and not

Power and authority rest with a person.

Lower status persons do not put forward ideas that conflict with leaders.

The chain of command is respected in South America.

to be passed over or ignored. As in the United States, they often screen people and projects before they ever get to the intended person. Take the time to visit with your counterpart's secretary. Bring a small gift, and ask about his or her family.

MEETINGS

Meet with top executives first. The group you meet with, at least initially, is normally determined as much by status as by competence. Your group should include at least one high-ranking member of your company who has the power to make decisions. Top South American executives may excuse themselves from subsequent meetings, which will take place with middle-level management and technical people. Don't feel insulted; this shows that discussions are proceeding positively.

Your host will direct you to your seat. Expect approximately ten to fifteen minutes of small talk to occur before getting down to business. This time is very important and should be used to develop a personal relationship with your South American counterparts.

If a South American group contains two or more top-level people who have the same amount of authority, there may be some intra-group disagreements at the meeting. Make sure you know who holds the power to make decisions so as not to waste time with someone who can't affect the decision and will ultimately accept whatever is decided. That's not to say, however, that those in positions of lesser authority are powerless. They can employ more indirect methods to influence their superior's decision if they are convinced that it is in their company's best interest.

The South American concept of "order" is different from that of North Americans.

The South American concept of "order" is different from that of North Americans. South Americans have a more circular notion of order and will discuss more than one thing at a time—and may interrupt a meeting to attend to other matters. What North Americans view as intrusions—personal matters and other supposedly "unrelated" topics of conversation—South Americans view as part of a larger whole.

PRESENTATIONS

South Americans speak with gestures, emotion and a lot of voice inflections. Expressiveness and emotion in presentations are viewed positively. A quiet, soft-spoken presentation without gestures may appear perfect and professional elsewhere, but will be viewed as uninteresting in South America.

Expressiveness and emotion in presentations are viewed positively.

THE TELEPHONE

Most of us think the first impression is made when we meet someone face to face for the first time. However, very often our first impressions of a company or a person are made over the telephone. Often this impression comes from a person's receptionist, secretary or administrative assistant. So it is important for you and everyone in your office to know what people expect when communicating by telephone.

Some cultures are comfortable with picking up a phone and doing business with people they have never met and perhaps never will meet. Many cultures, however, are not, so keep the following rules in mind:

- Cross-cultural communication is much more difficult when you can't see the non-verbal clues inherent in body language. Watch out for misunderstandings.

- Try to learn some basic phrases necessary to gain access to someone who may speak your language.

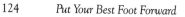

Watch out for misunderstandings.

- When calling, always identify yourself by name, position, company and country before asking to speak with someone. For example: "Hello, my name is Carrie Farrow. I am the international marketing representative for CMI and am calling from the United States. May I please speak with…"

- When greeting, apologize for not speaking their language if this is the case. Introduce yourself again.

- Don't be put off by people who answer the phone casually or carelessly.

- Always follow up a phone call with a fax, letter or e-mail summarizing your conversation and what, if anything, was decided. This is especially important when speaking to someone in a language that is not native to one of you.

South Americans are people-oriented. When phoning anyone from South America, never begin a phone conversation without first spending a few moments on personal issues. "How are you?" "How is your family?" "How is your weather?" "I understand you are busy preparing for Carnival." Never begin a conversation with "Did you get my fax?" Taking a few minutes to let people know you care about them will be well worth your time and effort.

Be aware: Figuring out how to make a phone call from another country without going bankrupt can be very challenging. Never direct dial a long-distance number or even pick up the phone in your hotel room without clearly understanding the costs. Get a phone card from your long distance telephone company and learn how to use it. You will save time, money and frustration.

Rule of Thumb

Always follow up a phone call with a fax, letter or e-mail summarizing your conversation and what, if anything, was decided.

South Americans are people-oriented.

A young woman told me about getting a super saver airline ticket from Detroit to France. She had a rip-roaring argument with her boyfriend at the airport the night she left. She felt so bad about the silly disagreement that she phoned him the moment she arrived at her hotel room in Paris. Making up, of course, took more time than she had planned.

When she checked out of the hotel, her room charge was $180 and the phone charge was $695. Her round-trip airfare was $350: it would have been cheaper for her to fly home, make up with her boyfriend, and fly back to France!

WRITTEN COMMUNICATION

- Don't judge intelligence based upon your counterparts' grammar or English language skills. Remember that they are probably communicating in a second language.

Don't judge intelligence based upon your counterparts' grammar or English language skills.

- Try using your counterpart's language in salutations and closings. End with a personal closing.

- Don't use acronyms (FYI, ASAP) or abbreviations: nite (night), 4 (for), U (you). Be especially watchful for this in your e-mail, since North Americans have come to regularly use these informal shortcuts in electronic communication.

- If a message evokes a negative emotion, defer an immediate response—or call the sender for clarification and more personal communication. Avoid "Nasty-Gram" warfare.

- If in doubt, use a formal writing style rather than informal.

- Know the hierarchy of the organization and who is appropriate to copy. Ask if you don't know. Avoid pre-set copy lists.

E-MAIL

Despite economic and technological obstacles, nonprofit and commercial groups in South America are joining the *superautopista de información*—the information superhighway. However, getting on this highway for South Americans may come at a high price. Many countries pay twice to three times as much money for thirty times less bandwidth. Equipment may cost up to 40 percent more than in the United States.

Internet popularity in North America and Western Europe has triggered a frenzied rush to provide commercial services such as Internet access and Web site posting in South America. There are now dozens of Internet providers and prices have plunged.

Avoid "Nasty-Gram" warfare.

Nonprofit and commercial groups in South America are joining the superautopista de información.

NEGOTIATION

The "take the money and run" style with no effort to develop a long-term relationship is an image of the North American businessperson that still lingers in South America.

Never rush negotiations.

- Never rush negotiations.

- Don't give up easily. You may be regarded as not being serious.

- Prove your sincerity.

It may take a long time to be regarded as a trusted friend, but once you are it's for life and will be a vital advantage to your business.

COMMUNICATION TIPS

- Try to arrange a "face to face" conversation if at all possible. Video conferencing can work very well when in-person communication is impossible.

A "hard sell" won't work in South America.

- Criticism must be handled delicately. Be indirect in order not to embarrass. South Americans may view faint praise as criticism. Praise should be effusive.

- A "hard sell" won't work in South America.

What sells in St. Paul may not sell in São Paulo—or it may sell very well, but need to be packaged, advertised, and marketed differently.

- Keep your message simple.

- Certain human needs and emotions cross all cultures. Appeal to the basics.

- Colors, music, body language and gestures all have different meanings in different cultures. Check the meaning and significance of these before you produce an ad campaign.

- Check whether the country is ad literate. There is an art to understanding assumptions made in ads. Countries that are just getting used to ads may not understand subtle cues.

- Every culture wants its uniqueness recognized. You may need to be culturally specific if you hope to sell to a niche market.

- Be careful in translating ads. A simple, inoffensive ad in one culture may be insulting and embarrassing in another. Hire two translators—one to translate the ad into the other culture and another to translate it back into English. Make sure you're saying what you want to. Have a cultural analyst proof your ad.

Rule of Thumb

Keep your message simple.

"THE MAGIC WAND"

It may appear that Disney World, a place of enchantment and wonder, has waved its magic wand and made a major cultural problem disappear.

Tens of thousands of Brazilians visit Disney World in Orlando, Florida, every year. It is almost a rite of passage for well-to-do Brazilian teenagers. The problem: Ebullient teenagers clad in soccer shirts surged through the park causing North American tourists and Disney World employees to complain: "Brazilians stand too close. We feel our space is being invaded." "Brazilians kiss and embrace a lot. We prefer to shake hands." "Brazilians are not accustomed to tipping." "Many of the Brazilian visitors break into lines."

Disney decided to promote understanding.

Disney decided, rather than criticizing or complaining, to promote understanding. They produced a video on how to behave at a United States theme park and sent it to travel agents in Brazil. Seminars were held in Brazil with more than 2,000 tour agents attending. At Disney World itself, special "leader-training programs" were introduced for guides and more Portuguese-speaking staff was hired.

Was it successful? "Absolutely," Disney spokeswoman Vicki Johnson said. "Even the bus drivers are saying they've noticed the difference."

Perhaps we could all learn a lesson from Disney's experience—and learn to wave the "magic wand" of cultural understanding ourselves.

- Appearance counts in South America. Staying in a good hotel and hiring a car will say to your present or potential customers and associates that you are already successful.

- Bill in advance. This is important with currency fluctuations.

- Be prepared to commit to the long term.

- Hire a local contact. This is invaluable, as South Americans may resent an outside representative.

- Breeding, background and family are important to South Americans. Yours may be scrutinized. Your education, who you know and where you're from counts. Skills can be learned; personal qualities cannot.

- You may confront some machismo when dealing with South American men. Such men respond to aggression, heroism and chauvinism rather than logic, persuasion and consensus. Business leaders are generally well educated, powerful men who are less likely to behave with machismo.

- Efficiency is second to a person's feelings. South Americans want to work for and with someone they can trust.

Appearance counts in South America.

Efficiency is second to a person's feelings.

A German company opened a manufacturing facility in a large South American city. During the initial training session, one of the South American women asked her German boss if she could be excused from a meeting early to take her daughter to the doctor. The German manager, while not happy about the woman bringing her personal life into her work, answered with a curt "yes." The woman left disgusted and determined to find a new job.

The German thought he was being very culturally sensitive while the South American couldn't imagine anyone being so insensitive as to not ask what was wrong with her child.

BE AWARE

NUMBERS

South Americans use a comma in the place of our decimal point, and a period in the place of our commas when writing numbers.

U.S.	South America
$1.00	$1,00
$100.00	$100,00
$1,000.00	$1.000,00

DATES

The date precedes the month.

Example: April 5, 1998 is written 5/4/98

TIME

North Americans who have done business in Europe or Asia will appreciate not having to reset their body time when traveling to South America. We are in the same time zones.

Be aware that South America generally uses the 24-hour clock, especially in hospitals, airports and businesses. For example: 2 p.m. is 14:00. Just add twelve hours to the time on your watch to get afternoon and evening times in the South American system. Morning times are the same.

SEASONS

Remember your gradeschool geography lessons? The seasons are reversed in the southern hemisphere. South America's summer is North America's winter, and vise-versa.

• Pack clothing appropriate for the season.

• When scheduling business trips, keep in mind that South Americans take their summer vacations in January and February.

HOLIDAYS AND FESTIVALS

Each South American country has special holidays and holy days on which businesses close. There are national days that are observed by everyone, but there are also regional festivals and holidays throughout each country in South America.

There are typical vacation periods during which it is impossible to do business. Avoid traveling to South America for business in January and February (remember, this is their summer!), Christmas and New Year's holidays, and Carnival (the week before Ash Wednesday). Check before scheduling a trip to a particular region. If you plan to drop in on customers or shop in the city, a local holiday may ruin your plans.

17.
ESPECIALLY
FOR WOMEN

Women have always been the dominant figures in South American private life as the managers of households. Now, although prejudice exists and women may still have to deal with the "glass ceiling" and machismo, the role and place of women in South American society is changing.

The role and place of women in South American society is changing.

Increasingly, women are seeking educational and career opportunities. Growing numbers of women in urban areas work outside the home. Young and upper- and middle-class females are active in business, government and the professions—many as doctors, lawyers and teachers. Every South American country has women who are in high-level government positions, nationally respected professionals and business owners.

The well-educated and traveled women generally detest "macho" behavior.

South American men are still "macho." Some women don't mind. Some even enjoy it. However, the well-educated and traveled women generally detest macho behavior.

MISS WORLD

South American women look stylish, attractive and most of all very feminine for all occasions—work or play. They are known worldwide for their beauty. Three of the five finalists in the 1997 Miss World Pageant were from Colombia, Venezuela and Brazil. Four recent Miss World winners were from Venezuela.

GENERAL RULES

- Research local cultural habits toward women and, even if you think they are silly or antiquated, respect them. Remember you are not in South America to "re-educate" the people or teach them to be "politically correct" a la North American style.

Be professional, but don't overdo it by being too brisk and impersonal.

- Establish your position and ability immediately. If possible, be introduced by a mutually respected person. Define your role clearly.

- Be professional, but don't overdo it by being too brisk and impersonal. Few things turn off South Americans more than aggressive, "non-feminine" women. Be warm and friendly but never lead anyone on or engage in unprofessional or sexual behavior.

- Dress in a feminine style, without flaunting your sexuality.

- Allow men to open doors, light cigarettes and otherwise be gentlemanly.

- Try not to become embarrassed or angry if someone addresses you in a manner you consider too personal. Roll with the punches.

- Your male business colleagues or customers may pay great attention to you and may compliment you and even flirt with you. While you may not be comfortable with this type of interplay between the sexes in business environments, it is part of the culture in South America. Graciously accept and enjoy the banter. It is normally extended as a friendly gesture with no disrespect intended.

Allow men to open doors, light cigarettes and otherwise be gentlemanly.

- At business meals, arrange payment with the restaurant beforehand if it is important for you to host the meal. Many South American businessmen will feel obligated to pay or be embarrassed if a woman pays. Some may be insulted if they are not allowed to do so.

- In many countries, it is traditional to invite someone for a drink after work. This should not be viewed as a come-on.

- Men (especially those of working class origin) may comment to you while you are in public. Just smile and keep walking.

- Accept *piropos* graciously. Loosely translated, *piropos* are flirtatious comments—there is no English word that quite captures this tradition! An example: "I wish I was a sidewalk, so you could walk on me." When thus complimented, just smile, keep walking, and say, "Thank you very much."

- Expect cultural misunderstandings over interaction between genders; try not to be judgmental. It may be new for some people to do business with women—be patient.

While having lunch with a female North American banker and her visiting colleague from Chile, I asked the Chilean how many times people from her country kiss when meeting and leaving. "Once for business meetings and twice for social meetings," she told me. The North American woman, working in a business environment in which employees are concerned about sexual harassment, was shocked that people would kiss at all in business situations. The Chilean woman saw nothing wrong with this, however, and expressed regret that coworkers in the United States, as she saw it, act so coldly toward one another.

18.

HEALTH AND SAFETY

If possible, visit a travel clinic—often found at university hospitals and major metropolitan medical centers—before a trip to South America. Most primary care physicians simply aren't familiar with health problems in and immunization requirements for other countries.

Make sure that your medical insurance covers you while you are in South America. If not, it is advised to take out a short-term supplemental policy. If you will be in remote areas, supplemental medical evacuation assistance is also advised.

Most South American countries do not require shots to enter, especially if you will be in the major cities. However, if you plan to visit the remote areas, especially in or near jungles, beaches or forests, you should check with the CDC fax information service (listed below). Immunizations against diphtheria, tetanus, polio, typhoid and hepatitis A may be

Rule of Thumb

Make sure that your medical insurance covers you while you are in South America.

recommended. If you are traveling to an area known to be infected with yellow fever, a vaccination certificate is required.

The standard of health care available at hospitals in South America varies from excellent to non-existent. As a general rule, check with your hotel personnel when dealing with a minor medical problem. If you even suspect your medical or dental problem is serious, call your embassy before seeking treatment.

If you even suspect your medical or dental problem is serious, call your embassy before seeking treatment.

HEALTH TIPS

• Pack a small first aid kit.

• Take your physician's phone number with you.

• Take all prescription and non-prescription medications you may need with you. Keep all medication in original, labeled containers to make customs processing easier.

• Remember that some hospitals require immediate payment for health services.

• Always wear shoes. Never walk barefoot on grass, cement, hotel room floors, etc.

• Wash your hands with soap before eating or putting them near your mouth.

- Drink only bottled water or water that has been boiled for twenty minutes, regardless of where you are visiting. While the water might be clean, even the different chemicals used to purify water could make you ill. Avoid ice cubes.

- If you can't peel it or have it safely cooked, don't eat it.

- Diarrhea is potentially dangerous. If symptoms persist, seek medical assistance.

- Malaria is found in some rural areas of South America, particularly those near the southwest coast. If you intend to be in these areas, consult your physician. Travelers to all coastal areas should always use insect repellent and take precautions to minimize contact with mosquitoes.

- Altitude sickness may affect you in some South American cities. Symptoms include lack of energy, a tendency to tire easily, shortness of breath, occasional dizziness and insomnia. You may need a short adjustment period. Minimize your consumption of alcohol. Take very special care if you decide to work out at high altitudes.

- Another risk at high altitudes is sun exposure. You can burn very quickly and severely in the thinner atmosphere. Wear

Drink only bottled water or water that has been boiled for twenty minutes.

Altitude sickness may affect you in some South American cities.

sun block as well as protective clothing, and minimize your exposure.

TOILETS

In good areas toilets are excellent and conform to Western standards. However, you may not always be in a good area, restaurant or hotel. My suggestion: If you come upon a good, clean facility, use it. You may not find another when you need it.

- Some restrooms in South America will display a sign requesting you place used toilet tissue in bins rather than the toilet bowl. It is very important that you honor this request in order for the system to function. You will not be popular if you ruin the sewage system in your host country.

- Carry tissues and handi-wipes with you in case they are not available.

- Always have small change available to tip the restroom attendant.

Smarte Carte keeps you moving.

TOILET TERMS

English	Portuguese	Spanish
Bathroom	Casa de Banho	Los Servicios or Baño
Ladies	Senhoras	Damas
Men	Homens	Caballeros
Hot water	Água quente	C (for *caliente*, "hot")
Cold water	Água fria	F (for *frío*, "cold")

SAFETY

Whenever traveling, be sure to take all the safety precautions you would at home. There are potential dangers in any city in the world.

South Americans are concerned about the safety of their guests. They will go out of their way to make you aware of the local dangers. Don't be afraid to ask them if there are any particular precautions you should take while visiting.

SAFETY TIPS

- Do not look or act like a tourist.

- Attempt to travel with at least one other person.

- Never travel anywhere you have been advised not to go by your hosts or hotel personnel.

There are potential dangers in any city in the world.

- Always avoid dark alleys and marginal areas, and be very careful in crowds.

- Petty thievery, pick pocketing, etc. are serious problems in some areas. Be alert.

- Be very alert to unusual incidents— a person fainting, dropping money, a stranger chatting familiarly with you, etc. It could be a staged distraction to allow pick pocketers to maneuver.

- Avoid wearing flashy jewelry and easily accessible valuables. Do not flash a lot of money.

- Take a taxi after dark. Phone for taxis from your hotel or location, or have the hotel doorman hail one for you. Try to avoid hailing one yourself.

- Be cautious when using mass transit. Ask about safety. Take a taxi or hire a car if possible.

- Walk at a distance from the curb to avoid thieves on motorcycles.

- It is not wise to carry anything that might be construed as a weapon; many areas have strict laws banning such items.

DRIVING

Make every attempt not to drive in South America. Taxis, hired cars and buses are readily available almost everywhere. Not only can driving be dangerous, but in several countries you have no legal rights if you are involved in an accident. My best advice for driving in South America is *don't*. If you can afford it, a car hired from your hotel is the best and safest means of transportation.

My best advice for driving in South America is don't.

ALTO

A friend of mine asked a South American gentleman what the word "alto" means in Spanish. She was very confused because it didn't seem as though anyone stopped at the red octagonal signs that read "alto." The gentleman, trying to be helpful, said, "Well, literally alto *does mean stop, but in reality it is really more of an advisement than a rule."*

RESOURCES

U.S. DEPARTMENT OF STATE

- Hotline for country-specific travel warnings: 202-647-5225 or 202-647-0900.

- Computer bulletin board: 202-647-9225, 9600/N/8/1

- World Wide Web: http://travel.state.gov.

CENTERS FOR DISEASE CONTROL AND PREVENTION (CDC)

- Health advisories, information on specific diseases and immunizations.

- Traveler's Hotline: 404-332-4559 or 404-639-2572.

- World Wide Web: http://www.cdc.gov/travel/travel.html.

- Fax Information Service: 404-332-4565. Dial this number and follow the prompts to get a list of international travel documents. Tropical South America: (10 pages) 220170. Temperate South America: (7 pages) 220180.

WORLD HEALTH ORGANIZATION (WHO)

- Current information on diseases, immunization requirements worldwide.

- 011-41-22-791-2111 (Geneva, Switzerland).

- World Wide Web: http://www.who.ch/welcome.html.

U.S. DEPARTMENT OF TRANSPORTATION

- Problems with airline bumping, charter flights, baggage and non-smokers rights.

- FAA Consumer Hotline: 800-322-7873.

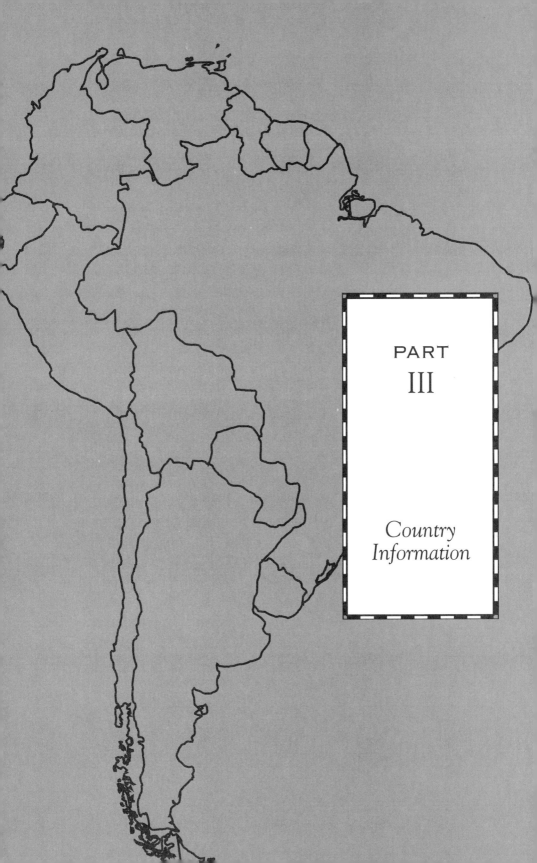

PART
III

*Country
Information*

North
Atlantic
Ocean

N

VENEZUELA

GUYANA

SURINAME

FRENCH GUIANA (FRANCE)

COLOMBIA

ECUADOR

BRAZIL

PERU

BOLIVIA

PARAGUAY

South
Pacific
Ocean

ARGENTINA

URUGUAY

CHILE

South
Atlantic
Ocean

FALKLAND ISLANDS
(Islas Malvinas)

The boundaries and city locations of this and the following maps are not intended to be geographically accurate.

19.
ARGENTINA
ARGENTINE REPUBLIC

VITAL STATISTICS

POPULATION: 33,913,000. Population distribution is very
uneven. About one-third of the population lives
in Buenos Aires and one-quarter lives in the
Pampas (the grasslands of central Argentina).
The dry Patagonian plateau in the south and the
wooded region *(Gran Chaco)* have few people.

CAPITAL: Buenos Aires, with a population of 12 million, is
one of the most populated areas in the world.
Buenos Aires, modeled after Paris, means "good
air" and is nicknamed "Baires" (BY-rays).
Residents of Buenos Aires are called *"Porteños,"*
which means "people of the port."

MAJOR CITIES: Córdoba (984,000), Rosario (957,000).

GEOGRAPHY:	1,068,000 square miles (2.8 million square kilometers), about the size of the United States east of the Mississippi River. Argentina is the second largest South American country after Brazil. It extends from the Antarctic in the south to the tropics in the north, the Atlantic on the east to almost the Pacific in the west.
GOVERNMENT:	Federal Republic, composed of 23 provinces and one federal district. The chief of state and head of government is the president, who is assisted by the vice president and cabinet. The National Congress is comprised of the Senate (72 members) and the Chamber of Deputies (257 members). The voting age is 18.
ECONOMY:	Argentina has long been one of the most developed nations in South America. Before World War I, Argentina was the sixth richest nation in the world. The Argentine economy is on a fast track to again becoming one of the world's strongest, helped by a small population and abundant natural resources. Inflation was a serious problem a few years ago, but it has stabilized under the current government.
LIVING STANDARD:	GDP = US$8,470 per capita.
AGRICULTURE:	Argentina is world-renowned for its livestock, particularly its exceptional beef. Other principal crops include sugarcane, soybeans, corn, wheat, flaxseed, grapes, sorghum, sunflower seeds,

potatoes, tomatoes, oils, cattle, sheep and roundwood.

INDUSTRY: Foodstuffs, meat packing, motor vehicles, consumer goods, textiles, metal products, chemicals, petrochemicals, printing, steel, paper, sugar, beer and tourism.

NATURAL
RESOURCES: Very rich in natural resources, including uranium, silver, gold, lead, zinc, tin, copper, iron ore, manganese and petroleum.

CLIMATE: Generally temperate, but varies from subtropical to sub-Antarctic.

CURRENCY: Nuevo peso argentino. 1 peso = 100 centavos.

Since April 1991, when the exchange rate became established by law, the nuevo peso has been maintained evenly with the U.S. dollar. This was a reaction to inflation and acts as a deterrent to financing public debt by printing money. U. S. currency is widely accepted. Change is not used very often.

THE PEOPLE

CORRECT
NAME: Argentines.
                 Adjective: Argentine.

ETHNIC
MAKEUP: 85 percent European, 15 percent mestizo.
                 European immigrants hail from Italy, Spain,
                 Austria, France, Germany, Great Britain, Portugal,
                 Russia, Switzerland, Poland and the Middle East.
                 Argentina has few indigenous people.

VALUE
SYSTEM: Argentines are very proud of their country and
                 culture. They are well-educated and sophisticated
                 and want to be viewed as cosmopolitan and
                 progressive. Argentines identify with Europeans and
                 may look down on North Americans and other
                 South Americans. It has been said that Argentines
                 are a nation of Italians who speak Spanish and
                 think they're British living in Paris. Personal
                 relationships are very strong. People are very
                 concerned with the consequences of their behavior.

FAMILY: Family and extended family are highly valued,
                 and personal identity comes from the family.
                 Families hold conservative values.

RELIGION: 93 percent Catholic, 2 percent Protestant, 1
                 percent Jewish, 4 percent other.

Many Catholics do not practice their religion, but people of all ages go to church on Sunday. Many consider it bad luck not to pray. Argentina has the strongest Jewish community in South America.

EDUCATION: Primary education (seven years) is compulsory and most people finish secondary education as well. Public schools and universities are free. The literacy rate is about 96 percent, one of the highest rates in South America.

SPORTS: Soccer (*fútbol*) is the national sport and very popular. Argentina's national soccer team participated in the 1994 World Cup tournament and won the World Cup in 1986 and 1978. When the team is in the World Cup, the whole country takes a holiday and streets are deserted—even government offices and utilities are shut down. U.S. football is called *"fútbol americano."* Horse racing, rugby, field hockey, tennis, polo and basketball are also popular. *Pato* is a sport in which riders on horseback attempt to toss a six-handled ball into a high basket. Argentina's polo players are some of the best in the world.

RECREATION: Musicals, nightclubs, dances, theater, outdoor picnics, barbecues and golf are popular. Teatro Colón, in Buenos Aires, is one of the finest opera houses in the world. The tango, which originated in Argentina, is a favorite of young and old. Indian folk music and classical music are also popular.

IMPORTANT DATES

Pre-16th
century
: Populated by Native American tribes. The Incan empire controls the northern part of present-day Argentina.

1580
: Spain establishes a permanent colony on the present site of Buenos Aires.

1810
: Rebellion against Spanish colonial government. General José de San Martín emerges as a hero in the fight for independence.

1816
: Argentine independence.

1853
: New constitution, strong central government.

1862
: Argentina becomes unified.

1916
: Radicals win control of the government and institute reforms on elections. Political processes open to the middle class and others previously excluded.

1930
: Military coup deposes radicals.

1946
: General Juan Domingo Perón becomes president during the general instability that follows a 1943 army coup. Perón's wife, Eva, works for women's rights.

1947
: Women given right to vote.

1955
: Military deposes Perón.

1973
: Perón returns from exile and maintains presidency for ten months before he dies. His second wife, Isabel, assumes presidency, becoming the first woman to head a national government in the Western Hemisphere.

1976	Mrs. Perón ousted by military. Civil War (Dirty War) begins; thousands of civilians die or disappear.
1982	Argentina seizes the British Falkland Islands. Britain wins the short war that follows.
1983	Dr. Raúl Alfonsín heads new civilian government.
1989	Carlos Saúl Menem, son of Syrian immigrants, becomes president in peaceful elections.
1993	Congressional elections give strong victory to Menem's party.
1999	Presidential elections scheduled to take place.

ARGENTINE FACTS

- Argentina means "silver."

- Some Argentines eat beef at all meals.

- Argentines hate taxes. There have been years in which only one percent of Argentines filed a tax return.

- Argentine women spend an average of $400 for underwear per year—twice as much as the world average.

- Buenos Aires has the largest ratio of psycho-analysts per capita of any city in the world.

- The highest and lowest points in South America are in Argentina, less than 100 miles apart. Aconcagua in the Andes is 22,834 feet high (the highest point in the Western Hemisphere) and Salinas Chicas, a salty region, is 138 feet below sea level.

More beef is eaten per capita in Argentina than anywhere in the world.

MEETING AND GREETING

See pages 63-67.

- A handshake and nod show respect when greeting someone.

- An embrace and one kiss on the cheek is common between friends and acquaintances.

- Some older people might kiss twice.

See pages 69-75.

NAMES AND TITLES

- Titles are valued and used often.

- Use your Argentine colleagues' academic titles.

LANGUAGE

- Spanish is the official language and is spoken by 95 percent of the population.

- Argentines speak the dialect of Castile, Spain. Argentines say "Hablo castellano" instead of "Hablo español" for "I speak Spanish." They use "vos" instead of "tú" for "you," and "sos" instead of "eres" for "you are."

- Italian has heavily influenced Argentine Spanish, which has distinct words, phrases and pronunciations not found in other Spanish-speaking countries.

- *Lunfardo* is Argentine slang, a mixture of Spanish with Italian, French and English.

Italian has heavily influenced Argentine Spanish.

- Many people speak English, especially in main tourist centers. Because of the large European population, Italian, German and French are also widely spoken. Several indigenous languages are used as well.

- Learn as much Spanish as possible. Even a few phrases will be appreciated.

BODY LANGUAGE

- Argentines are touchers. It is common to see women holding hands and men with arms around each other.

- People stand close when speaking. Do not back away, even if you are uncomfortable with the close space.

- Do not speak with your hands on your hips.

- Cover your mouth when you yawn or cough.

People stand close when speaking.

- Do not sit on a table or ledge or prop your feet up on a table, chair or desk.

GESTURES

- Moving your hand from under your chin means "I don't know."

- Twisting your index finger to your temple indicates "crazy."

- Hitting the palm of your left hand with your right fist means "I don't believe what you are saying" or "That's stupid."

- The "O.K." and "thumbs up" gestures are considered vulgar.

- In many cafes, make a cup with your fingers if you want a cup of coffee.

- Eye contact in conversation is essential.

- Talk about soccer, history, culture, the opera, international travel, North American jazz and the tango, which originated in Argentina.

- Talk about Buenos Aires, its beauty, sophistication and how it is so European!

- Ask about and compliment children.

- Compliment Argentine wine, a national pride.

- Do not talk about Great Britain or the Falkland Islands (Las Malvinas to the Argentines). Argentina claims ownership of these islands.

Do not talk about Great Britain or the Falkland Islands.

- Be careful when discussing the Perón years. People either love or hate the Peróns; there is no middle ground.

- Although Argentines may discuss politics and religion very vocally, avoid adding your opinions to these discussions.

See page 80.

PHRASES

DINING AND SOCIAL EVENTS

- The main meal is served at noon, but the evening dinner may also be large. Dinner never starts before 9:00 p.m. and may begin at 10:00 p.m. or later on weekends.

- Tea or coffee and pastries are often served between 4:00 and 6:00 p.m. This is modeled after the English tea time.

- Never use a toothpick, blow your nose or clear your throat at the table.

- Meals are for socializing. Never discuss business during a meal.

- Address a waiter as Señor and a waitress as Señorita. To summon a waiter, raise your hand with your index finger extended. Although a local may make a kissing noise to attract a waiter, this is an impolite gesture that you should not imitate.

Order Argentine wine, which is excellent and a source of national pride.

- Do not order imported liquor unless your host does. Taxes are exorbitant. Order Argentine wine, which is excellent and a source of national pride.

- Avoid pouring wine, which is a complex ritual in Argentina.

- Eating in public is inappropriate. Do not eat in the street or on public transportation.

FOOD

- Tender beef and wonderful wine are the pride of Argentina. North American beef and wine are considered inferior.

- Barbecues, consisting of beef, beef, beef, lamb and more beef, are a favorite recreation. Gauchos barbecue whole cows. A vegetarian will be about as popular in Argentina as in Texas.

- Beef is preferred over fish, chicken or lamb, although chicken is becoming more acceptable.

- Pasta and fresh vegetables are very popular.

TYPICAL FOODS

- *Carne asada*: beef steak.

- *Asado*: barbecue.

- *Asado con cuero*: beef roasted in its hide over an open fire.

- *Empañadas*: pastries stuffed with a combination of meat, chicken, ham, seafood, eggs, olives, vegetables, raisins and cheese.

"Six restaurants in the world can prepare a perfect steak. Four are in Argentina."

—Smith & Wollensky,

—a famous New York steakhouse

- *Pucheros*: stews.

- *Locro*: a winter stew of meat, corn and potatoes.

- *Maté*: the national beverage. Maté is a tea brewed from the dried leaves of a native holly tree. It is a mildly narcotic drink that is sipped through a straw from a gourd or peel of fruit. Sharing maté is a cultural ritual showing friendship. It is very popular in homes and on picnics, but rarely served in restaurants.

TIPPING

- Tipping is not required, but is becoming customary in restaurants. Tip ten percent if there is not a service charge, five percent otherwise.

- It is optional to tip taxis. If your change is less than fifty centavos, don't ask for it.

- Tip hotel porters and doormen US$1.

DRESS

- Argentines are extremely fashion conscious.

- Dress well if you want to make a good impression. Your clothing will be scrutinized, and you will be judged by your appearance.

- Argentines do not wear modest or subdued clothing.

- Women are expected to dress with a flair that does not detract from their professionalism.

- Some cultural dress is popular in outer regions. Do not attempt to wear any native Indian costumes or native outfits.

BUSINESS

- Men: Conservative, dark suits and ties.

- Women: Suits, skirts and dresses.

EVENING/ENTERTAINMENT

- Men: Dark suits, often with an ascot in place of a tie.

- Women: Dresses and skirts.

CASUAL

- Men: Nice pants with a blazer or jacket.

- Women: Older women wear skirts and dresses. Younger women dress more casually and are beginning to wear pants.

- Clean, neat designer jeans are worn by everyone.

Do not attempt to wear any native Indian costumes or native outfits.

GIFTS

- Do not give personal items, including clothing.

- When presented with a gift, open it at once and be appreciative.

HOSTESS

- Give flowers, candy, pastries, chocolates and imported liquor, which is very expensive in Argentina.

BUSINESS

- Business gifts are not expected until a fairly close relationship has been formed. Gifts are not necessarily reciprocal.

A very expensive gift may be interpreted as a bribe attempt.

- High-quality gifts will be appreciated. A very expensive gift may be interpreted as a bribe attempt.

- Give high quality scotch, books and gifts which discreetly display your company's name or logo.

- A small gift to secretaries is appreciated.

DO

- Be prepared for Argentine humor which may mildly attack your clothing or weight. Don't be offended by this friendly banter.

- Read *The Buenos Aires Herald*, an excellent English-language newspaper.

- Carry plenty of one and five peso notes. Few stores have change for over twenty and few taxis for over ten.

- Always greet officials before asking them questions.

- Learn the tango—even a few steps will be appreciated. The tango originated in Argentina and is the national dance.

DO NOT

- Do not bring up the Falkland Islands War. When discussing the islands, remember the Argentine name: Malvinas Islands or Las Malvinas.

- Do not praise the countries neighboring Argentina. Wars have been fought with all of them.

Learn the tango— even a few steps will be appreciated.

- Never compare Argentina with the United States or Brazil, which is considered a rival.

- Argentines are very sensitive to criticism.

PUNCTUALITY AND PACE

- Argentines don't like to get up early or be rushed.

- Argentines believe "the person is more important than the hour."

- For social events, arrive thirty to sixty minutes late. To arrive at a party on time would be impolite.

- Be on time for lunch appointments, the theater and soccer.

- Be punctual for business appointments, but prepare to wait thirty minutes for your counterpart, especially if you are meeting an important person. The more important the person, the longer the wait.

- Ask "*¿En punto?*" ("On the dot?") if you are uncertain about timing for a business appointment.

- The pace of business in Argentina is slower than in the United States. A meeting that is going well could last much longer than intended, even if it means postponing the next engagement.

CORPORATE CULTURE

- Argentina is a very bureaucratic and litigious country.

- Personal relationships are more important than business relationships, and a relationship must be built before business is done.

- Education, professional contacts and wealth influence social and business prominence.

- Decisions are made at the top. Attempt to meet the top person in the organization.

MEETINGS

- Argentines often need several meetings and extensive discussion to make deals. Making several trips will be beneficial.

- Guests at a meeting are greeted and escorted to their chairs. The visiting senior executive is seated opposite the Argentine senior executive.

- Be prepared for small talk. It is customary to spend up to half an hour discussing everything but business.

- Sustain a relaxed manner, maintain eye contact and restrict the use of gestures.

It is customary to spend up to half an hour discussing everything but business.

COMMUNICATION

- The negotiation pace is slower than in the United States and the style is relaxed. Don't take a hard sell approach.

- Argentines are tough negotiators, and concessions will not come quickly or easily. Good relationships with counterparts will shorten negotiations. Try not to change representatives during negotiations.

- Contracts will be lengthy and detailed. Signing a portion of the contract is not final until the entire contract is signed. Any portion can be re-negotiated.

- Get everything in writing.

- E-mail is an acceptable form of communication, but don't expect a quick response.

BE AWARE

- Never criticize anyone, especially in public.

- You will need an Argentine contact to get through to the highly bureaucratic government.

- Argentinians often view people from the U.S. as naive and slow to grasp new ideas.

Never criticize anyone, especially in public.

ENTERTAINMENT

- Take the time to socialize and develop friendships. Socializing is an essential part of doing business.

- Business dinners are for socializing and developing relationships, although some business might occur. You shouldn't initiate business talk, but your Argentine colleague might. The conversation will mix business and social topics.

- Business dinners are generally held in restaurants. When you are the host, arrange payment ahead of time. If this is not possible, insist on paying—you'll have to do it more than once.

- Imported liquor is very expensive. Never order it if you are a guest.

APPOINTMENTS

- Make your contacts and appointments through a high-level person, whom your Argentine contact can help you find.

- You can make appointments by mail, but the postal service is considered unreliable— be careful of what you mail.

- Confirm meetings one week in advance.

Take the time to socialize and develop friendships.

Make your contacts and appointments through a high-level person.

BUSINESS HOURS

- Businesses are generally open from 9:00 a.m. to 5:00 p.m. Monday through Friday and 9:00 a.m. to 1:00 p.m. on Saturdays in Buenos Aires. In other cities, businesses may be open 9:00 a.m. to noon and then 2:00 p.m. to 7:00 or 8:00 p.m.

- Banks are open from 10:00 a.m. to 3:00 p.m. in the east and from 8:00 a.m. to 1:00 p.m. in the west.

- Most government offices are open from 9:00 a.m. to 5:00 p.m.

- Many Argentine executives work until 10:00 p.m. A business meeting at 7:00 or 8:00 p.m. is not uncommon.

ESPECIALLY FOR WOMEN

Machismo is still very strong but is being challenged by women who are now highly visible and influential in politics and business. Argentine businesswomen are at a level similar to that of North American businesswomen.

- Most men respect women in business, but some may be chauvinistic and make it difficult for a foreign woman.

- Argentine men are very friendly and easy to get along with. They show great interest in women. If you smile and invite conversation, you have a friend for life.

- *Piropos*—flirtatious comments—are common. Men may call out "Hey, gorgeous!" while you're walking down the street. When thus complimented, just smile, say "Thank you very much," and keep walking.

- Defensive behavior will damage your credibility. Emphasize status and responsibility.

- A kiss and hug is considered a compliment to a woman.

- Buenos Aires has modern facilities and the water is generally safe. Modern facilities are less reliable in other regions of Argentina.

- Malaria is present in rural areas.

- Buenos Aires is safer than most big cities. It is safe to walk about at night, but be alert— muggings do occur. Watch for pickpockets and purse-snatchers.

- Crossing the street in Buenos Aires is impossible. Traffic does not wait for or give the right of way to pedestrians.

HEALTH AND SAFETY

Buenos Aires is safer than most big cities.

HOLIDAYS AND FESTIVALS

Do not plan to make a business visit or schedule any appointments during the following holidays or festivals. Be sure to check for the numerous regional and local holidays and festivals.

January	New Year's Day (1)
March/April	Holy Thursday (varies)
	Good Friday (varies)
May	Labor Day (1)
	First National Government, Independence Day (date of actual break with Spain) (25)
June	Malvinas Day (10)*
	Flag Day (20)*
July	Independence Day (formal, written break with Spain) (9)*
August	Anniversary of the death of General San Martin (17)
October	Columbus Day (12)
December	Feast of the Immaculate Conception (8)
	Christmas Day (25)

* celebrated the closest Monday

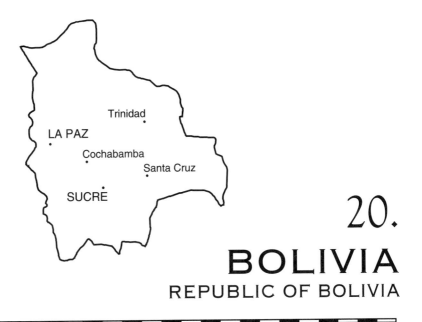

Trinidad

LA PAZ

Cochabamba

Santa Cruz

SUCRE

20.
BOLIVIA
REPUBLIC OF BOLIVIA

VITAL STATISTICS

POPULATION: 7,900,000. About half the population is rural.

CAPITAL: The official capital is Sucre with a population of
                100,000. However, most business and
                government offices of interest to international
                visitors are in La Paz (1,057,000).

MAJOR CITIES: Santa Cruz (628,000), Cochabamba (381,000).

GEOGRAPHY: 420,163 square miles (1,090,581 square
                kilometers), about the size of Texas and
                California combined. Bolivia has four
                geographical areas. The *Altiplano* in the west lies
                between two ranges of the Andes and is high,
                cold and dry. 40 percent of Bolivians live in the
                Altiplano, many in La Paz. The *Yungas* in the

northeast are of medium elevation, consisting of steep hills and narrow gorges. The *Valles* are gently sloping hills and broad valleys in the south, where much of the country's food is produced. The *Oriente*, a vast lowland plain over north and east Bolivia, consists of tropical forest and open grasslands.

GOVERNMENT: Republic, composed of nine departments and one federal district. The president is both the chief of state and head of government. The National Congress consists of the 27-seat Chamber of Senators and the 130-seat Chamber of Deputies. Voting is mandatory for everyone beginning at age 18.

ECONOMY: Hampered by political instability and the lack of a seaport, Bolivia has been one of the poorest countries in South America. Economic figures have improved since Peru granted Bolivia access to the sea through the Ilo port in southern Peru. Market-oriented reforms and free-market policies in the last ten years have also provided a boost to the economy.

LIVING
STANDARD: GDP = US$784 per capita.

AGRICULTURE: Sugarcane, bananas, rice, potatoes, plantains, corn, cassava, soybeans, wheat, barley, sorghum coffee, quinine, pork, cattle, goats and sheep.

Coca, the substance used in making cocaine, is the largest cash crop. Because coca has many medicinal and dietary uses in the Bolivian culture, it is very difficult for the government to stop coca trafficking.

INDUSTRY: Manufacturing, mining, textiles, foodstuffs, chemicals, plastics and petroleum.

NATURAL
RESOURCES: Tin, natural gas, petroleum, zinc, tungsten, antimony, silver, lead, gold, iron ore, timber and fish.

CLIMATE: Varies with altitude, from humid and tropical to semi-arid and cold.

CURRENCY: Boliviano. 1 boliviano = 100 centavos.

THE PEOPLE

CORRECT
NAME: Bolivians.
Adjective: Bolivian.

ETHNIC
MAKEUP: 30 percent mestizo, 30 percent Quechua, 25 percent Aymara, 15 percent European.

VALUE
SYSTEM: Bolivians are kind, gentle people, who are concerned for each other's welfare. Friendship is a very important value. Self-identity is based on the social system and the history of the extended family.

It is difficult to define classes according to ancestry in Bolivia. Generations of intermarriage have created large numbers of mestizos in all classes. There is some tension between the classes. To assimilate into society, people must speak Spanish and adopt Western ways. Some indigenous people have even taken Spanish names to be accepted. The situation has improved over the last several years, and Bolivians take great pride in this progress.

FAMILY:

The family is the central unit in the social system. Children are generally well trained and disciplined. Many elderly live with their children. Most women are homemakers.

RELIGION:

95 percent Roman Catholic, 5 percent other.

The church has a great moral influence and gives a sense of stability in life. Catholicism is the official religion, but freedom of worship is guaranteed by law. Many Catholics hold various Indian religious beliefs and honor traditional Indian gods.

EDUCATION:

Education is valued but still not achievable for all people. Although it is legally compulsory for ages six to fourteen, fewer than half of all children finish primary education. Educational reforms have helped indigenous children by allowing bilingual education in Spanish and local Indian dialects. The literacy rate is 80 percent.

SPORTS:	*Fútbol* (soccer) is the most popular sport. The Bolivian national soccer team competed in the 1994 World Cup.
RECREATION:	Music is a Bolivian passion. Dancing and singing are popular. The Bolivian national dance is the *cueca*, danced by couples waving handkerchiefs. Visiting friends and family, watching television and attending local festivals are popular pastimes.

IMPORTANT DATES

10,000 years ago	American Indians inhabit the area of modern-day Bolivia.
14th century	The Aymara, a warlike tribe, control western Bolivia.
13th century	The Incans defeat the Aymara and make Bolivia part of their huge empire. The Incans force their customs, religion and language, Quechua, on the Bolivian Indians.
1530s	Arrival of the Spanish.
1809	War of Independence begins, lasts sixteen years.
1825	Bolivia declares independence from Spain, led by liberator Simón Bolívar.
1828	The first president is overthrown. Decades of strife, revolution and military dictatorships follow.

1884	Bolivia loses Pacific Ocean ports to Chile.
1935	Bolivia loses oil-rich Chaco region to Paraguay.
1951	Reform government of Dr. Víctor Paz Estenssoro elected.
1952	National revolution.
1964	Estenssoro government overthrown by military; reform ends. A series of coups and oppressive dictators follow.
1980	Terrible economic conditions and spiraling inflation (peaking at 11,700 percent) end military government.
1982	Dr. Víctor Paz Estenssoro reinstated by a democratic election. Economy stabilizes and inflation rate falls to 20 percent.
1988	War with coca growers.
1989	Peaceful election of Jaime Paz Zamora.
1993	Peaceful election of Gonzalo Sánchez de Lozada.
1997	Presidential elections scheduled in May.

- Bolivia was named after Simón Bolívar, the revered hero of South American independence.

- Bolivians are very proud of being one of the few countries that have successfully promoted multicultural integration. Vice President Víctor Hugo Cárdenas, elected in 1993, was the first indigenous person elected to this high office in South America.

- The world's highest ski run, highest golf course, highest navigable lake, highest airport with scheduled service and highest city are all in Bolivia.

- Butch Cassidy and the Sundance Kid were killed in Bolivia after a bank robbery.

- Ché Guevera, the communist revolutionary, tried to start a revolt in Bolivia in the mid 1960s. He was killed by Bolivian troops in 1967.

- The Aymara language is so precise that Japanese computer scientists have used it as a model while developing computer languages.

- Bolivia has lost more than half of its territory since independence in wars or treaties with Argentina, Brazil, Chile, Paraguay and Peru.

Vice President Víctor Hugo Cárdenas, elected in 1993, was the first indigenous person elected to this high office in South America.

MEETING AND GREETING	See pages 63-67.
	• The customary greeting is a handshake. Shake hands when meeting and departing.
	• Close male friends may embrace. Female friends embrace and touch cheeks.
	• Bolivians kiss twice, once on each cheek.

NAMES AND TITLES	See pages 69-75
	• Titles are very important. Learn your counterparts' titles and use them correctly.

LANGUAGE	• The official languages are Castellano Spanish, Quechua and Aymara.
	• Spanish is the mother language of about 40 percent of the population. Spanish is spoken in government, schools and business. Most people you meet in the business community will speak Spanish.
	• Indigenous people speak their own languages.
	• Bolivian Spanish is very correct, without slang.

- Bolivians stand very close when conversing.

- You will be viewed as untrustworthy if you do not maintain direct eye contact. This may be difficult if your Bolivian counterparts stand very close, but it is essential in conversation.

- Correct posture while sitting and standing will be noticed. A slumping posture is rude.

- Never sit on a table, desk or ledge.

- Cover your mouth if you must yawn or cough. Never whisper to anyone.

GESTURES

- The "so-so" gesture (rocking your palm-down open hand from side to side) means "no" in Bolivia. Bus and taxi drivers use this to indicate that their vehicle is not for hire and street vendors use it to show they are sold out of something.

- Waving an index finger means "no."

- Beckon a child by making a scooping motion with your palm down. Never beckon an adult with this motion.

- Making a fist with the thumb protruding between the index and the middle finger— the "fig" gesture—is rude.

Correct posture while sitting and standing will be noticed.

SMALL TALK

- Bolivians love to talk. Conversation will be lively.

  - Talk about family, food, soccer and auto racing.

  - Know something about Bolivian sports. It will be appreciated.

  - Don't talk about poverty, religion, drugs or the United States' drug policy. The United States' military activity in Bolivia is a sore spot with many citizens.

- Do not give political opinions on Bolivia.

- Never praise Chile, Brazil or Paraguay. Bolivia has lost wars with and land to all its neighbors.

- Make an effort to use Spanish in conversation—it will be appreciated.

Do not give political opinions on Bolivia.

PHRASES

See page 80.

- Breakfast usually consists of tea or coffee, bread and sometimes cheese.

- Lunch is the main meal and includes soup and a main course.

- It is common to have tea and cakes around 4:00 p.m.

- A full evening meal is usually eaten around 9:00 p.m.

- Decline the first offer of food—wait until your host insists.

- Never touch food or eat anything with your fingers. Even fruit is eaten with a fruit knife and fork. Keep your hands above the table, not in your lap.

- It is polite to eat everything on your plate.

- Complimenting the food will be viewed as a request for more. Wait until the dinner is over if you don't want more.

- Never leave the table until everyone is finished.

- Stay at least 30 minutes to one hour after dinner is finished.

Complimenting the food will be viewed as a request for more food.

- The host usually insists on paying for the meal in a restaurant.

- Never eat while walking in the street.

FOOD

- Potatoes, which originated in Bolivia, are the main staple. There are many varieties prepared in many different ways.

- Many Bolivian foods are very spicy. Salsa is commonly served.

- Bolivians love barbecues.

- *Paceña* is a very famous Bolivian beer. It is so good that Germans export it to Germany.

Many Bolivian foods are very spicy.

TYPICAL FOODS

- *Quinua:* a grain, often made into a soup and eaten by the poorer people.

- *Humintas:* corn-filled pies.

- *Salteñas:* meat or chicken pies with potatoes, olives and raisins, enjoyed midmorning in the cities. They are a famous Bolivian specialty.

- *Chuños:* freeze-dried potatoes added to soup or side dishes.

- *Pasankhalla*: popcorn, which originated in Bolivia.

- *San-Pedro*: a white grape liquor made in Bolivia. It is served at every party, regardless of the class of the host.

- *Coca*: Coca has been used for thousands of years, and Bolivians make a sharp distinction between coca and cocaine. Coca leaves are used to make a tea which people believe will help you combat altitude sickness, cure a bad stomach and give a person great energy. Among the lower class, friends may offer each other coca tea or a wad of coca leaves to chew as casually as North Americans offer each other coffee.

TIPPING

- A 10 percent tip is generally included in the bill at an expensive restaurant, but leaving a little extra (up to 5 percent) is polite. There is no manditory 15 percent.

- Always ask the cost of a trip before you enter the taxi.

- It is customary not to tip taxi drivers, except for long trips. They generally own their own vehicles.

- Tip porters US$1 per bag.

DRESS

- Be prepared for a variety of climates. The lowlands are subject to hot, humid summers, and comfortable cotton clothing is recommended. Bring a sweater for evenings in high altitude cities.

Be prepared for a variety of climates.

- Do not wear Indian clothing, including bowler hats. The native Indians may think you are making fun of them.

- Women are not expected to wear nylons during the summer, even for business attire.

BUSINESS

- Men: In La Paz, a dark three-piece suit is best. A lightweight suit is more common in Santa Cruz. Follow your Bolivian colleague's lead with regard to wearing ties and removing jackets in the summer.

- Women: Suits, dresses, skirts and blouses.

EVENING/ENTERTAINMENT

Do not wear shorts in cities.

- Follow the same rules as for business.

CASUAL

- Clean, fashionable jeans and pants are appropriate casual wear for both men and women.

- A gift given sincerely will be appreciated regardless of the value. The intention is what counts.

- Gifts may not be opened by the recipient until after the giver has left.

- Gifts from the United States, particularly from your region, are appreciated.

HOSTESS

- Give flowers, wine, whiskey and high quality chocolates.

- Don't give yellow or purple flowers. Purple is the color of death.

- Bring a bag of assorted North American candy (Tootsie Pops, candy bars, etc.) for children. It will be very well received.

A gift given sincerely will be appreciated regardless of the value.

BUSINESS

- Give high quality pen and pencil sets, office organizers, books and art from the United States and your home region.

- If your company logo is on a gift, it should be small and understated.

- Bolivians are very social people. They enjoy meeting with friends and visiting.

- It is customary to drop by unannounced as a way of showing someone you are thinking of them.

DO

- Refer to Indians as *campesinos* (farmers), not *indios*.

- Bolivians appreciate people who are warm and friendly.

- Ask to taste a *salteña*. These are delicious meat pies that were introduced to Bolivia by two women from Argentina. Do not visit Bolivia without tasting these great creations.

Bolivians are very social people.

DO NOT

- Never flaunt your wealth. Bolivian people tend to appreciate simplicity. They want to be respected for who they are, not what they have.

- The United States' drug policy is a touchy subject with Bolivians. They believe North Americans should educate their children about drug abuse instead of interfering in the national policies of Bolivia. They feel blaming a Bolivian coca farmer for drug problems is like blaming an Iowa grain farmer for alcoholism. Regardless of your opinion, this is a subject best avoided.

PUNCTUALITY AND PACE

- Although punctuality is not a high priority in Bolivia, visitors should be punctual for business meetings.

- It is impolite to show up on time to a social occasion. Guests are expected to be fifteen to thirty minutes late for dinner or parties.

It is impolite to show up on time to a social occasion.

- Business meetings rarely start on time.

- If you want to ask a Bolivian if they expect you to be prompt, you can ask "*¿En punto?*" ("On the dot?").

STRICTLY BUSINESS

CORPORATE CULTURE

- Take the time to get to know your Bolivian customers and colleagues. Personal relationships are vital to your corporate success.

- Deadlines are not considered important.

MEETINGS

- More than one meeting will be necessary to negotiate and close a deal. Plan on taking several trips to complete your business, since face-to-face communication is preferred over phone calls, faxes and e-mail.

COMMUNICATION

- Translate printed materials into Spanish if possible, although many business executives speak English.

Take the time to get to know your Bolivian customers and colleagues.

- Bring an adequate number of business cards. Have them printed in Spanish on one side and English on the other.

- The pace of business negotiations is generally much slower than in the United States. Never attempt to rush a deal. Applying pressure will cause a deal to fail. Remain low-key.

- Presentations should be visual and appealing.

- E-mail is becoming more and more popular and is an acceptable form of business communication. Do not expect an immediate response to your e-mail.

BE AWARE

- Appearances count. Stay at a prestigious hotel.

- Hire a local contact to assist you in the Bolivian business community. Third party contacts will be vital to your success.

- A contract is not finished until an agreement is reached on all parts. Each part is subject to re-negotiation until the entire contract is signed.

Appearances count.

- Try to send the same representatives to Bolivia each time. A new representative will have to start from scratch to build a new relationship.

ENTERTAINMENT

- Entertainment for businesspeople can be a luncheon or dinner in a restaurant. Spouses do not usually attend these events.

APPOINTMENTS

- Make appointments two to three weeks in advance.

- Make appointments for morning meetings, if possible.

- April through October are the best months to do business. Avoid making business plans during Carnival Week (the week before Ash Wednesday) and the weeks before Christmas and Easter.

Avoid making business plans during Carnival Week.

BUSINESS HOURS

- Businesses are generally open from 9:00 a.m. to noon and 2:00 p.m. to 6:00 p.m., Monday through Friday. Some business people keep office hours on Saturday mornings.

- Government offices hold the same hours as businesses, but often are open until 6:30 p.m.

- Banks are open from 9:00 a.m. to noon and 2:00 p.m. to 4:30 p.m.

- The midday break is called the *alnuerzo de hora,* and allows people to have a leisurely lunch and relax.

ESPECIALLY FOR WOMEN

Machismo is very strong in Bolivia, and women are considered subordinate. This puts severe restrictions on women's social and work behavior. Women have fewer economic opportunities than men.

- Women run and manage their homes. The work is difficult because many homes lack modern conveniences.

- When doing business with Bolivian men, emphasize your credentials and experience.

It is traditional for men to go out after work together on Friday nights to relax, drink a few beers and discuss sports, business and current affairs. Women do not object because they believe that the men are calmer and more caring on Saturday and Sunday after getting this out of their system.

HEALTH AND SAFETY

- Arrive a day early to adjust to the high altitude. Remember that high altitude increases the intensity of the sun's rays and the effects of alcohol consumption. Drink little or no alcohol until you become acclimated to the altitude. Be careful of sunburn.

- Sanitation facilities are poor and bottled water is recommended.

Arrive a day early to adjust to the high altitude.

- Most tourist areas are relatively safe, but there have been isolated terrorist attacks against U.S. officials and missionaries during the past few years.

- Be careful if you are traveling near centers of coca-leaf and drug processing areas.

- Carry your passport with you. Officials may stop you and if you don't have it, you will be taken to the police station and fined.

HOLIDAYS AND FESTIVALS

Do not plan to make a business visit or schedule any appointments during the following holidays or festivals. Be sure to check for the numerous regional and local holidays and festivals.

January	New Year's Day (1)
February/March	Carnival (the week before Ash Wednesday, varies)
March/April	Good Friday (varies)
	Easter (varies)
May	Labor Day (1)
June	Corpus Christi (varies)
August	Independence Day (6)
November	All Saints Day (1)
December	Christmas (25)

- Almost every Bolivian village has special fiestas with dancing, costumes and food. Many of these festivals honor the local patron saint or the Virgin Mary.

- Carnival, celebrated the week before Ash Wednesday, is everyone's favorite time. Dancing, music, costumes, favorite treats and throwing water on people are all part of the fun. Everyone participates.

Belém
Manaus
São Luís
Rio Branco
BRASÍLIA
Cuiabá
São Paulo
Rio de Janeiro
Pôrto Alegre

21.
BRAZIL
FEDERATIVE REPUBLIC OF BRAZIL

VITAL STATISTICS

POPULATION: 166,800,000, the fifth most populous country in the world. Ninety percent of the people live on 10 percent of the land in the relatively narrow coastal corridor. Fifty percent of the population is under age twenty.

CAPITAL: Brasília, with a population of 1,568,000.

MAJOR CITIES: São Paulo (10,063,000), Rio de Janeiro (5,603,000).

GEOGRAPHY: 3,286,473 square miles (8,511,965 square kilometers), the fifth largest country in the world. Brazil is about the size of the United States. Forests cover 65 percent of Brazil and include the world's largest tropical rain forest, the Amazon River Basin.

GOVERNMENT: Federal Republic, consisting of 26 states and one federal district. The executive branch consists of a president, vice president and cabinet. The bicameral National Congress is composed of the 81-member Federal Senate and the 503-member Chamber of Deputies. Brazil is considered one of the most stable democracies in South America.

ECONOMY: Brazil is the largest economy in South America and the tenth largest economy in the world. In the 1980s, national debt and inflation were rampant. Since 1992, however, inflation has dropped from 50 percent to approximately 2 percent. Economic reforms to stabilize the economy continue to be top priority.

Income distribution is very unequal: one-third of the population lives below the poverty line. Social programs aimed at decreasing poverty have been successful in recent years.

LIVING STANDARD: GDP = US$5,450 per capita. The GDP has more than tripled in the last twenty years.

AGRICULTURE: Bananas, oranges, coffee, soybeans, cocoa, corn, beef, sugarcane, wheat, beans, coffee, cotton, tomatoes, potatoes, peanuts, rice, beef, cattle, pork and rubber.

Brazil is the world's largest producer of oranges, bananas and coffee. More than half the orange juice purchased in the United States is from

Brazil. Brazil is the second largest producer of soybeans and cocoa, and the third largest producer of corn and beef.

INDUSTRY: Automobiles and auto parts, textiles, minerals, iron ore, steel, petrochemicals, machinery, consumer goods, cement, wood products, shipbuilding, tourism, metal products, fertilizer, foodstuffs, textiles, clothing, paper products, plastics and pharmaceuticals.

NATURAL
RESOURCES: Iron ore, manganese, bauxite, nickel, uranium, gems, petroleum, phosphates, tin, gold, platinum, timber, hydroelectric power, granite, limestone, clay and sand. Brazil generates most of its electric power from its hydroelectric dams.

CLIMATE: All of Brazil lies south of the equator and has mostly a tropical climate. Heat and humidity are common in the coastal and forest regions. More moderate temperatures are normal in the highlands (São Paulo).

CURRENCY: Real. 1 real = 100 centavos.

               During the last decade, Brazil has had at least six different currencies. The real replaced the cruzeiro in July 1994 as part of an anti-inflation program.

THE PEOPLE

CORRECT
NAME: Brazilians.
                   Adjective: Brazilian.

ETHNIC
MAKEUP: 53 percent European, 22 percent mulatto, 12
                   percent mestizo, 11 percent black of African
                   ancestry, 1 percent Japanese, 1 percent other.
                   There are 150,000 Native Americans in Brazil.

VALUE
SYSTEM: People are friendly, fun, warm and free-spirited,
                   with an incredible zest for life. They are very risk-
                   oriented and very creative, traits that helped them
                   survive years of unstable economic conditions.
                   Brazilians don't agonize about who they are—they
                   just don't think about it. They consider themselves
                   people from a great country and are completely at
                   ease with themselves. Class separation is observed.
                   The middle class, upper-middle class and elite live
                   completely apart from the working class. People are
                   not interested in ethnic background, but in
                   educational and family background.

FAMILY: The family unit is very strong. Families are large
                   and include extended family. Children rarely
                   leave home before they marry. Traditionally,
                   families are led by the fathers but mothers make
                   decisions regarding the home. It is unacceptable
                   to send the elderly to nursing homes, and the
                   infirm live with their children.

RELIGION:	73 percent Roman Catholic, 20 percent Protestant, 2 percent Afro-American Spiritual, 2 percent Spiritist, 1 percent atheist, 2 percent other.

Brazil has more Catholics than any other country in the world, and the Catholic church has had a great influence on society. Most Catholics, however, only attend church on special holidays. Catholics may not follow all Catholic beliefs regarding abortion, contraception, living together before marriage, etc. Some Catholics observe other religions as well. It is very common for a Catholic to attend Mass on Sunday and go to a *Macumba* (an African voodoo religion) ceremony on Friday.

EDUCATION: Education is compulsory to age fourteen, and approximately 40 percent of students attend secondary schools. Students cannot enter Brazil's top universities without passing special college preparation courses and difficult entrance exams. The literacy rate has risen from 66 percent to 82 percent in recent years due to a national adult literacy program.

SPORTS: Soccer *(futebol)* is the national sport, and children learn to play early. Brazil won the World Cup in 1994. Hundreds of thousands of fans jam huge stadiums to watch professional soccer games, and many businesses and schools close during important matches. Brazilians consider themselves the best soccer players in the world. Pelé (one of the world's best soccer players) and Emerson Fitipaldi (the

Formula One Grand Prix race car driver) are from Brazil. Other popular sports include basketball, volleyball, boating, fishing, swimming, auto racing and horse racing. People know and especially like NBA basketball from the United States.

RECREATION: Visiting family and friends is a favorite pastime. People enjoy many fine beaches on the east coast of Brazil and the well-to-do ski in beautiful mountain resorts. Brazilians are proud of their music. Dancing, especially the samba, is popular—everyone dances. Brazilians don't care for merengue or salsa. Religious and national festivals are very popular, and such events are celebrated with parades featuring decorated floats, costumes, street dancing, games and fireworks. The greatest festival is Carnival, celebrated the week before Ash Wednesday, when people from all over the world travel to Rio de Janeiro to join the festivities.

IMPORTANT DATES

Pre-16th Century	Native American tribes, including the Guaraní and Tupinambá, populate the area of modern Brazil.
1494	Treaty of Tordesillas divides the Americas between Spain and Portugal.
1500	Portuguese Admiral Pedro Álvares Cabral is the first European to reach Brazil and claims the area for Portugal on April 22.
1630	The Netherlands invades Brazil.

1654	Portugal drives the Dutch out of Brazil.
1808	The Portuguese monarchy, led by King Dom Joao IV, flees Napoleon's army and transfers the seat of government to Brazil from Lisbon. Rio de Janeiro becomes the seat of the Portuguese Empire.
1815	Dom Joao declares Brazil a kingdom, equal with Portugal.
1822	Dom Joao returns to Portugal. His son Dom Pedro declares Brazil an empire and himself emperor. He declares Brazil's independence from Portugal on September 7.
1888	Slavery of black Africans abolished.
1889	The second emperor, Dom Pedro II, is deposed by a military coup. Brazil is declared a republic.
1930	Military coup by Getúlio Vargas, who rules for fifteen years.
1946	A new constitution restores individual rights.
1960	Capital moved from Rio de Janeiro to the new city of Brasília.
1964	Military coup.
1985	Tancredo Neves appointed president by electoral college, dies after assuming office. Vice President Jose Sarney assumes office.
1988	Present constitution adopted.
1989	Fernando Collar de Mello becomes the first directly elected president in 29 years.
1992	Legislature calls for Collar's impeachment due to corrupt activities. Collar resigns. Itamar Franco becomes president.
1995	Fernando Henrique Cardoso, who had been in exile from 1964-1985, is elected President.

BRAZILIAN FACTS

- Eleanor Roosevelt shook her head and said "Poor Niagara" when she saw Iguaçu Falls.

- Brazil is considered the "lungs of the world" because of its huge rain forests.

- Brazil passed a law in 1997 making all Brazilians organ donors after death unless they specify otherwise.

- Brazil is an important center of New Age spirituality.

DIVERSITY

You will encounter every skin color and ethnic combination in Brazil. The great diversity of the Brazilian people is amazing! Some examples:

- *The largest community of Japanese outside of Japan lives in Brazil.*

Brazil has more Italians than Venice.

- *São Paulo has the largest community of Lebanese in the world, larger than the population of Lebanon.*

- *Brazil has more Italians than Venice.*

- *Confederate refugees from the U.S. Civil War formed a colony in Brazil in the latter half of the nineteenth century. Their descendants still live in Americana, just outside São Paulo, and hold an old-fashioned southern ball once a year.*

See page 63-67.

See page 63-67.

- Brazilian greetings are warm and friendly. Friends embrace. Women kiss women.

- Take time to greet everyone present. Be sure to say good-bye to everyone before leaving.

- Women kiss twice—once on each cheek— if they are married. A single woman adds an extra, third kiss.

MEETING AND GREETING

See pages 69-75.

- Brazilians move to a first name basis quickly.

NAMES AND TITLES

- The official language is Portuguese.

- English and French are common second languages. In hotels and restaurants, many people will speak English. English is the international language most frequently used by the business community. Businesspeople important enough to be meeting with foreign executives will probably speak English.

- Spanish is understood by most Brazilians, but not often spoken. Do not assume that your Brazilian colleagues speak Spanish. Try to speak a few words of Portuguese.

LANGUAGE

The official language is Portuguese.

- No local dialects are used widely, but a number of Brazilian words and phrases are different from the Portuguese used in Portugal.

BODY LANGUAGE

- Brazilians are warm, friendly, outgoing and emotional people. Physical contact is part of simple communication. Touching arms, elbows and backs is very common and acceptable.

Physical contact is part of simple communication.

- Brazilians stand extremely close, sometimes less than a foot away. Do not back away.

- Do not shove or push anyone in a crowd—although you may yourself be pushed.

- Never burp in public. It is terribly crass.

- Do not expect alot of kissing in business.

GESTURES

- The "O.K." sign is very rude and vulgar and could cause a fight.

- The "thumbs up" gesture is used for approval.

- A finger snap indicates something done in the past or a long time ago, as well as indicating "do it quickly."

- The "fig" gesture—tucking your thumb between your index and middle finger—indicates good luck.

- Wiping your hands together means "it doesn't matter."

- Clicking your tongue and shaking your head back and forth indicates disagreement or disapproval.

SMALL TALK

- Talk about soccer, family, Brazil's beautiful beaches, and the country's rapid growth in industry.

- Ask about your colleagues' children.

- Do not talk about politics, poverty, religion, Argentina (considered a rival) or the deforestation of Brazil.

- Even though Brazilians tell ethnic jokes (about Portuguese), don't participate.

- Never ask questions about personal topics such as age, salary, marital status or job.

However, don't be shocked if you are asked such personal questions.

- When talking about soccer, never refer to it as "soccer"—say "football" (*futebol*). United States football is referred to as "American football."

- Brazilians are expressive and passionate conversationalists. When they argue their points, they are not angry; it is just a style of communication. Be prepared to be interrupted. It is not considered rude, but rather interpreted as enthusiasm.

- Do not be surprised if someone asks your religion or political preferences.

PHRASES

See page 81.

DINING AND SOCIAL EVENTS

- Breakfast consists of coffee with milk (*café com leite*), fruit and bread with butter, cheese or marmalade.

- Lunch is the main meal of the day.

- Snacks (cookies, cake and beverages) may be served from 4:00 to 5:00 p.m.

- Dinner is late, 8:00 to 10:00 p.m., and is a light meal unless Brazilians are formally entertaining.

- People always wash their hands before eating and never touch food with their hands. Use a knife and fork for everything, even fruit. Always use a napkin while eating or drinking.

- Do not use a toothpick unless you cover your mouth with your other hand.

- To beckon a waiter, hold up the index finger of your right hand and quietly say "Garçon."

- To request the check, say "A conta, por favor." You will need to ask for the check. No one will bring a check or rush you to leave.

- You will always be offered coffee and a snack when visiting a Brazilian home. You may be invited to join a meal.

- Meals are more about socializing than food. Never finish dinner and leave. Stay at least an hour and a half after dessert.

- Don't go to a party hungry. An 8:00 p.m. party may not serve food until 9:30 p.m. or

Do not use a toothpick unless you cover your mouth with your other hand.

Meals are more about socializing than food.

later. Parties may continue until 2:00 a.m. or as late as 7:00 a.m. the next day.

- When inviting Brazilian friends for dinner or a party, do not suggest that your guests bring food or drink. Do not expect them to arrive on time, and never, never indicate a time that the party will "end."

FOOD

- Coffee (*cafezinho*) is Brazil's chief drink. It is very strong. North American coffee looks and tastes like "dirty water" to Brazilians.

- Brazilian barbecue (*churrasco*) is very popular. It is not served with sauce.

TYPICAL FOODS

- *Mate*: a kind of tea. In southern Brazil, especially Rio Grande do Sol, people drink it all the time. Cold mate is very common in Rio on the beaches.

- *Feijoada*: black beans with beef, pork, sausage, and tongue. It is Brazil's national dish.

- *Bife a cavalo com fritas*: meat with eggs and french fries.

- *Batidas*: a sweet fruit beverage made with rum.

- *Americano*: a sandwich made from ham, cheese, lettuce, tomato and a fried egg.

- *Aguardiente*: a brandy-like drink made from sugarcane.

- *Churrasco*: charcoal broiled meats, popular in southern Brazil.

TIPPING

- Ten percent is generally included in a restaurant bill. Add 10 to 15 percent if it is not included. Leave extra change if a service charge is included.

- Taxis are typically tipped 10 percent in Rio. Tipping is not expected elsewhere.

- Tip porters US$.75 per bag.

Brazilians do not like to deal with change, round up your bill to the nearest real.

DRESS

- Appearance counts! Your clothing will reflect upon you and your company.

- People are very fashion conscious and may even be ahead of Europe in style.

- Brazilian women dress sexily in all situations, whether business, formal or casual. Skirts are short, blouses are cut low and clothes are tight. Anything goes! Foreign women who want to blend in should avoid wearing overly formal, conservative attire.

- Shoes are noticed. They must be stylish, polished and well-kept.

- Nails and hands are noticed. Invest in a manicure.

- Avoid wearing green and yellow together. These are the colors of the Brazilian flag.

- Be prepared for rain. When it rains, it pours. The water rushes through the streets.

- Rio's beaches are not full of topless swimmers. Go to Buzios if you want to swim topless.

- The *fio dental* (dental floss) bathing suits are less common than they have been in the past. Some believe the more stable, conservative political climate has had something to do with this change. Now suits are *asa delta* (hang glider), covering the rear in a V shape.

BUSINESS

- Men: Conservative dark suits, shirts and ties. Three piece suits indicate executives; two piece suits indicate office workers.

- Women: Feminine dresses, suits and pantsuits. Don't "dress like a man."

EVENING/ENTERTAINMENT

- Men: Dark suits, shirts and ties.

- Women: Dresses, skirts and blouses.

CASUAL

- Men: Nice slacks and long-sleeved shirts.

- Women: Nice slacks, skirts and blouses.

- Jeans are acceptable if they are clean and fashionable, not torn and tattered.

Jeans are acceptable if they are clean and fashionable.

GIFTS

- Nice gift-wrapping will be noticed.

- Always open a gift in front of the giver. It is very insulting not to do so.

HOSTESS

- Send flowers before or after visiting someone's home for dinner.

- Flowers in any color are appropriate for the middle and upper classes. Do not give purple flowers to people of the lower class, who may be very superstitious. Purple is the color of death.

Always open a gift in front of the giver.

- Give candy, wine, champagne, scotch and Copenhagen chocolate (a very good quality candy made and sold in Brazil).

BUSINESS

- Gifts are not important in establishing a relationship, and people won't expect gifts in the first few contacts. A very expensive gift may be viewed as a bribe.

Gifts are not important in establishing a relationship.

- Present a gift at a social meeting, not during a formal business meeting.

- Give good quality whiskey, wine, coffee table books and name brand pens.

- Gifts for your counterpart's children will be appreciated. T-shirts, sweatpants and soccer paraphernalia are appropriate. NBA shirts and hats will be enthusiastically received.

HELPFUL HINTS

Brazil was colonized by Portugal, not Spain.

- Brazil was colonized by Portugal, not Spain. Brazilians are not Spanish.

- Brazilians are very different from and don't mix well with other South American cultures. There are no bad feelings, just an attitude of "why bother?"

- Brazilians think North American culture is a bit slow and funny. However, they like the people and products from the US.

- There is competition between Rio and São Paulo. Rio is considered the heart of Brazil and São Paulo is considered the pocketbook.

- The "self-made" businessperson is not admired in Brazil. Inherited wealth and a good family background are much more desirable. People refer to someone with a new Mercedes or new Persian rug disparagingly as "nouveau."

- Brazilians are proud of their bodies and work very hard to keep themselves fit. Everyone works out. Cosmetic surgery on every part of the body is common and popular.

DO

- Carry a copy of your passport with you for identification purposes. Keep the immigration permit given to you—losing it will result in a fine when you depart.

- If you are attending a *candomble* ceremony, ask permission before taking photos. Stay off the dance floor, which is a sacred place only for believers.

Carry a copy of your passport with you.

DO NOT

- Don't smoke in public. Federal law bans smoking in public places—including movie houses, theaters, restaurants, libraries and hospitals—except in special areas. In many places, it is also illegal to smoke on buses, in shopping malls and in restaurants, although enforcement has been lax.

Don't smoke in public.

- Don't refer to Brazilians as Latins.

- Don't make a fuss if you're in a line—and you will always be in line in Brazil!—and someone casually walks to the front, flashes a card, and gets served. VIPs and government officials are not only allowed but expected to do this. Rather than being angry, people in the queue will nod and say, "That must be a very important person."

PUNCTUALITY AND PACE

- Brazilians are extremely casual about time. Being ten to fifteen minutes late in business is normal, and twenty to thirty minutes late is not unusual.

Brazilians are extremely casual about time.

- Be on time for a formal meeting, but prepare to wait for your Brazilian colleagues. Brazilians are aware of North American punctuality and may make an effort to be on time for meetings with North Americans.

- Add extra time for traffic.

- People from São Paulo are more punctual than other Brazilians.

- When invited for a Brazilian lunch, dinner or party, never arrive on time. You are expected to be at least half an hour late. Arrive late for a party at someone's home— about one hour for parties and half an hour for dinner.

Events can begin hours later than their scheduled time. A North American businessman arrived at a Brazilian nightclub for the 10:00 show—and sat alone until 11:30, when people began to arrive for the show, which began at 1:00 a.m.!

STRICTLY BUSINESS

CORPORATE CULTURE

- The person doing business is more important than the company. Your personality will make more of an impression than the prestige of your company name.

- To succeed, you will need to commit long term resources in time and money and take the time to establish strong personal and business relationships.

- Brazilians will do anything for friends. They have an expression: "For friends, everything. For enemies, the law."

The person doing business is more important than the company.

Relationships are more important than a legal document in business.

- People from São Paulo are more formal, punctual and straightforward than other Brazilians. They approach business with an intensity and a zest.

MEETINGS

- Meetings are conducted at a casual, unhurried pace. Never get right down to business. Engage in conversation first.

- In São Paulo, meetings are more European and businesslike than in the rest of Brazil.

COMMUNICATION

- Having your cards printed in Portuguese on one side is a good idea, but English-only is acceptable.

- Speak English or Portuguese, or use an interpreter.

- Doing business with Brazilians requires face to face communication. You will be able to do only limited business by phone, fax or e-mail.

- Be patient. Negotiating a contract will take time and several visits.

- Never change your negotiating team.

- Some facts may not be completely accurate during the early stages of negotiations. Brazilians expect some initial hype.

- Be prepared to be interrupted during highly animated negotiations, with "no" being interjected often. Brazilians may appear angry when they passionately argue their points.

- Brazilians are great bargainers. They make concessions slowly and grudgingly.

- Always get a written agreement with a starting date, time of delivery, payment details, etc. Bill in advance.

- Presentations should be expressive and have some flair.

- It is acceptable to communicate via e-mail, but don't use it if you need an immediate response.

BE AWARE

- Stay at a first class hotel. Appearances count.

- Hire a Brazilian contact (a *despachante*) from your industry to introduce you to the right people. He or she will be invaluable to your success.

- Hire a local accountant and lawyer to help you with contract issues. Brazilians may resent an outside legal representative.

Be prepared to spend at least two hours at a business lunch.

ENTERTAINMENT

- Always entertain in a prestigious restaurant. Get a reference from your hotel concierge or your colleague's secretary.

- Be on time for business dinners, but be prepared to wait.

- Business entertaining is more commonly done in restaurants than in homes. Most business dinners are held in private clubs.

- Do not discuss business during meals unless your host brings it up. Business may occasionally be discussed at dinner in São Paulo or Rio.

- Be prepared to spend at least two hours at a business lunch.

- Business meetings are rarely held during breakfast.

APPOINTMENTS

- Make appointments two weeks in advance.

- The best times for appointments are 10:00 a.m. to noon and 3:00 p.m. to 5:00 p.m.

- Never "drop in" on business or government offices without an appointment.

- Do not attempt to do business around Carnival. Never try to get anything done on Ash Wednesday. The whole country is "hung over, sleeping or repenting."

BUSINESS HOURS

- Businesses are generally open from 8:30 a.m. to 5:30 p.m., Monday through Friday. Decision-makers may start later and work later.

- Banks are generally open from 10:00 a.m. to 4:30 p.m.

- Stores and businesses never close at noon.

Rule of Thumb

Never try to get anything done on Ash Wednesday. The whole country is "hung over, sleeping or repenting."

As women increasingly join the workforce, machismo has become less common. Younger and better-educated women have values that correspond closely to those of North American women. Women are well accepted and respected and are prominent in education, medicine, journalism and as small business owners.

- The relationship between the sexes is very free and open in Brazil. Men may ask for a date—and get it—while stopped in traffic. Many romances have begun in traffic jams in Rio.

- Brazilian women are very aggressive, in both their business and personal lives. They are much more free and open than in other South American countries.

- Foreign women will usually have no problem doing business in Brazil. However, some people are still conservative in this regard.

- Be very careful not to ruin a business deal by being cool and too professional.

- It is not considered rude to stare at women and make comments as women pass by.

- It is traditional to invite someone for a drink after work. This is not a come-on.

Brazilian women can be very aggressive romantically, and forward to the point of harassment. Do not be surprised if you are in a restaurant or nightclub and a woman sends you a note asking for your phone number. This is referred to as a "torpedo," and it may happen even if you are with your wife or girlfriend. Foreign men traveling in Brazil should be very cautious when dealing with Brazilian women. If you don't want the attention, be cordial but keep your distance. Never be overly friendly.

HEALTH AND SAFETY

- Yellow fever, typhoid and cholera immunizations are recommended if you will be traveling outside urban areas.

- Wear mosquito repellent at all times.

- Never eat unpeeled or uncooked fruits or vegetables. Drink bottled water.

- Traffic is chaotic and fast. Brazilians consider traffic laws to be "advisements" rather than rules. Observe the traffic for a few days before attempting to drive—or, better yet, don't drive at all.

- Watch before crossing the street—drivers don't slow down for yellow lights.

Never eat unpeeled or uncooked fruits or vegetables.

SAFETY GUIDELINES

Violent crimes against tourists have become much less common than in the past, in large part due to the efforts of the Brazilian tourist police. Visitors can avoid being victimized with some simple safety guidelines:

- Make sure your hotel is insured against theft if you are leaving valuables in a safe.

- Don't leave your hotel wearing jewelry, even a watch.

- Don't flaunt cameras, jewelry or money. Look out for your money and documents.

- Theft is a problem at airports—keep an eye on your luggage.

- After dark, take a taxi rather than walk.

- Watch for pickpockets.

- Some areas are very dangerous. Listen to the advice of your Brazilian colleagues on where you should and should not go.

Theft is a problem at airports— keep an eye on your luggage.

Watch for pickpockets.

Do not plan to make a business visit or schedule any appointments during the following holidays or festivals. Be sure to check for the numerous regional and local holidays and festivals.

January	New Year's Day (1)
	St. Sebastian Day (Rio only) (20)
	Foundation of the City (São Paulo only) (25)
February/March	Carnival (the week before Ash Wednesday, varies)
	Shrove Tuesday (the day before Ash Wednesday, varies)
March/April	Easter (varies)
April	Tiradentes Day (21)
May	Labor Day (1)
June	Corpus Christi (varies)
September	Independence Day (7)
October	Day of the Patroness of Brazil (Our Lady of Aparecida) (12)
November	All Soul's Day (2)
	Proclamation of the Republic (15)
December	Christmas (25)

- Oktoberfest is celebrated in a ten-day festival in the southern town of Blumenau.

- On New Year's Eve in Rio, Copacabana Beach has a celebration where residents dress all in white and throw women's objects—lipstick, flowers, mirrors, etc.—into the sea for the sea goddess, Iemanja.

Arica

Valparaíso •. SANTIAGO

Concepción

Puerto Montt

Punta Arenas

22.
CHILE
THE REPUBLIC OF CHILE

VITAL STATISTICS

POPULATION: 14,500,000.

CAPITAL: Santiago, with a population of 5.5 million. About
                one-third of Chileans live in Santiago.

MAJOR CITIES: Concepción (294,000), Valparaíso (294,000).

GEOGRAPHY: 292,257 square miles (756,942 square
                kilometers), larger than Texas. Chile is 4,022
                miles long—the distance from San Diego to
                Charleston—but averages only 100 miles in
                width. The widest point is only 250 miles across.

GOVERNMENT: Republic, composed of thirteen regions. The
                president is the head of government and cannot
                be re-elected for two consecutive terms. The

National Congress has two houses: the 46-member Senate and the 120-member Chamber of Deputies. Several political parties are officially represented in the government. The voting age is eighteen, and all eligible citizens are required to vote by law.

ECONOMY: Chile's economy has shown outstanding performance for several years. In the last ten years, Chile has become the model for economic change for the entire region by being the first country to open its doors to foreign capital, slash tariffs, liberalize investments and privatize state enterprises. The economic "miracle" has not stinted social programs. While overall public spending was cut, social spending increased by 61 percent in 1995. The result: a 30 percent cut in the poverty rate and illiteracy reduced to 5 percent.

LIVING
STANDARD: GDP = US$5,680 per capita. Incomes of the poorest Chileans have risen by 20 percent since 1980.

AGRICULTURE: Fresh fruit—apples, grapes, peaches, nectarines—is becoming Chile's main agricultural export. Other products include sugar beets, wheat, potatoes, corn, rice, oats, rapeseed, barley, onions, beans, sheep and cattle.

INDUSTRY: Cement, cellulose, fish products, iron, steel, paper products, beverages, tires, pulp, glass, petroleum products, metal products, foodstuffs and lumber.

NATURAL
RESOURCES: Copper, timber, fish, iron ore, nitrates, precious metals, molybdenum, manganese, zinc, silver and gold. Chile is the largest worldwide producer of copper, which accounts for 50 percent of its exports.

CLIMATE: Chile has many different climates varying greatly with latitude. The north is subtropical, the central region moderate, and the south is subarctic. The central, temperate regions have four seasons, similar to the United States.

CURRENCY: Chilean peso. 1 peso = 100 centavos.

THE PEOPLE

CORRECT
NAME: Chileans.
               Adjective: Chilean.

ETHNIC
MAKEUP: 95 percent European (Spanish, German, Yugoslav, Italian, French) and Indian mixed (mestizo), 3 percent Native American, 2 percent other. Chileans do not draw attention to or discuss race.

VALUE SYSTEM:	Chileans are law-abiding, pragmatic people who believe in progress. They are optimistic and confident about the future. Respect and courtesy are important, especially to the elderly. People are judged by their education and family background, not by race. Money is not important as a screen of acceptance, and a strong middle class exists. They are very nationalistic and proud of their country.
	Chileans have always been kind, humble, hardworking people. While neighboring countries have accused Chileans of arrogance and cockiness since their economic "miracle," Chileans themselves encourage a self-deprecating humor. One recent television ad by a major company showed a sharply dressed Chilean man making a grand entrance at a posh party—and then slipping and tumbling down a flight of stairs.
FAMILY:	Family is the primary structure of society. Families eat meals together, and social functions always include several generations. The father is still considered the head of the family, but the mother is an important decision-maker. Being from the "right" family can determine a person's success. Just having a name from the upper class will get a person in the door almost anywhere.
RELIGION:	89 percent Roman Catholic, 11 percent other, including various Protestant groups and a small Jewish minority.

Church and state are separate, and religious freedom is guaranteed by the constitution. For Catholics, regular attendance at mass is not common or considered important.

EDUCATION: Chileans are proud of their literacy—the 95 percent rate puts them among the best educated in the world. Schooling is compulsory from six to fourteen years of age. Education is valued as a way to improve life, and university degrees are highly regarded.

SPORTS: *Fútbol* (soccer), swimming, skiing (both water and snow), fishing, tennis, rugby, golf, basketball, roller hockey and kite flying are popular sports.

RECREATION: Chileans dance the cumbia, tango, waltz and rock but not the merengue or salsa. The cueca is a very beautiful national dance that is traditionally performed on National Day (September 18) by dancers dressed in ponchos, boots and black hats. Music is played by Spanish guitars and a harp.

IMPORTANT DATES

Pre-16th Century	Incans rule the northern part of modern-day Chile. Mapuche and Araucano Indians inhabit the south.
1536	Diego de Almagro claims Chile for the Spanish Empire.

1541	Spain conquers Chile despite native resistance.
1810	Chile proclaims independence from Spain.
1817	Bernardo O'Higgins, the independence hero who is considered the "George Washington of Chile," becomes the first president. He is deposed in 1823.
1879-1884	War of Pacific against Peru and Bolivia. Chile wins and annexes the provinces of Arica and Antofagasta.
1880s-1932	Periods of government instability and military interventions ended by elections held in 1932.
1964	Eduardo Frei Montalva is elected president and institutes economic and social reforms, nationalizing some foreign-owned companies.
1970	Salvador Allende Gossens becomes the first freely elected Marxist president.
1973	General Augusto Pinochet Ugarte leads military coup, initiating seventeen years of military rule.
1988	Pinochet loses a plebiscite confirmation of presidential powers until 1997.
1989	First democratic elections since 1970. President Patricio Aylwin Azocar takes office in 1990.
1994	President Eduardo Frei Ruiz-Tagle is elected.
1999	Presidential elections scheduled.

- Chile is known as the "Switzerland of South America" for its incredible natural beauty.

- Chile is a true "melting pot" of ethnicities. Chileans ask proudly, "Where else in the world can you find German immigrants who speak Spanish and revere a national hero named O'Higgins?"

- Two Nobel Prize winners in literature have come from Chile. The first Latin American to win the literature prize was Gabriela Mistral in 1945 for her verse and prose. Pablo Neruda won in 1971 for his poetry. Both express beautifully the dreams and frustrations common to many South Americans.

Chile is known as the "Switzerland of South America."

See pages 63-67.

MEETING AND GREETING

- Chileans are very warm and expect visitors to reciprocate. They may be formal at first but move to friendship very quickly.

- A handshake, a warm hug and one kiss on the right cheek are common greetings among friends.

- Always greet the head of the household first.

Chileans are very warm and expect visitors to reciprocate.

NAMES AND TITLES	See pages 69-75
	• Titles are not as commonly used or as important as in other South American countries.

LANGUAGE	• Castellano Spanish is the official language, spoken by 95 percent of the population. Mapuche, a native language, is spoken by 4 percent. Minorities speak other languages, including German and Italian.
Make an effort to speak Spanish—it will be appreciated.	• Santiago has a large English-speaking population. English is the most studied foreign language and is understood by many in the large cities.
	• Make an effort to speak Spanish— it will be appreciated.

BODY LANGUAGE	• Eye contact and correct posture are important during conversation. They indicate an interest in the other person's opinion.
	• Smiles are greatly appreciated.
	• Never back away, even if you are uncomfortable with someone's proximity. Chileans stand closer than North Americans do.

- Cover your mouth with your hand when coughing, sneezing or if you can't suppress a yawn. Excuse yourself.

- Never toss items at people—pass politely.

- When smoking, offer a cigarette to everyone. Chileans have a saying, "Did you learn to smoke in jail?" for those who neglect to share.

GESTURES

- Never click your fingers to or at anyone.

- Never beckon with your index finger.

- A chin flick means "I couldn't care less." This is not used by educated people.

- Hitting the palm of your left hand with your right fist is a vulgar gesture.

Hitting the palm of your left hand with your right fist is a vulgar gesture.

SMALL TALK

- Expect to be interrupted. This is not considered rude, but rather a way of showing interest and enthusiasm.

- Talk about history, cuisine, wine, travel, sports, geography and the economy, which Chileans are very proud of.

Expect to be interrupted.

- Show interest in and talk about family, especially children.

- It is acceptable to ask a person's occupation, but do not ask about salaries.

- Do not talk about politics or human rights, especially as a foreigner, unless your host initiates the discussion.

- Do not refer to anyone as a "mestizo." It is considered insulting.

PHRASES

See page 80.

DINING AND SOCIAL EVENTS

- Breakfast is served between 7:00 and 9:00 a.m. "A continental" breakfast is coffee or tea with toast and juice or fruit.

- The main meal is eaten between 1:00 and 3:00 p.m.

- Tea time (*onces*) is from 5:00 to 6:00 p.m. It consists of beverages, small sandwiches and pastries.

- Dinner is eaten between 8:00 and 10:00 p.m., and is generally a light meal.

- Correct European-style table manners are vital. It is very important to know which flatware to use. Forks and knives should be used for everything eaten at a table.

- Keep both hands above the table at all times, never on your lap.

- Never make smacking noises with your mouth or silverware.

- Don't lick your fingers or use toothpicks, which are considered vulgar.

- Water is not automatically served at the table. Ask for a glass if you want some.

- Taste everything that is served. Compliment the host or hostess on the meal.

- Conversation is free, friendly and open at the table, but do not speak with food in your mouth.

- Never leave immediately after dinner. Stay for conversation after the meal.

- An invitation for drinks at a private home generally includes dinner. Call to thank or send a thank-you note after a dinner in someone's home. This is not customary in Chile, but it will be appreciated. Guests should reciprocate with comparable hospitality at a later time.

- Barbecues are popular social gatherings.

- Summon a waiter by raising your hand.

- You will not be presented with a bill in a restaurant until you ask for it.

- There are no separate checks—the person who invites pays. Arrange in advance to pay the bill in a restaurant if you are the host.

FOOD

- Seafood is abundant and outstanding.

- Chile is famous for its excellent wines. Ask about and enjoy the wine, which is a source of national pride.

TYPICAL FOODS

- *Asados:* grilled beef.

- *Empañadas de Horno:* baked turnovers filled with meat, hard-boiled eggs, onions, olives or raisins.

- *Pastel de Choclo:* meal of beef, chicken, onions, corn, eggs and spices.

- *Cazuela de Ave:* chicken in broth with vegetables and potatoes. It is eaten in two steps: first drink the broth, then eat the meat and vegetables.

- *Sopaipillas:* deep-fried pumpkin dough, a particular favorite of children, especially on rainy days.

- *Humitas:* a flat pancake made from ground corn and stuffed with corn paste. They can be made sweet or salty.

TIPPING

- Tip 10 percent in restaurants if a tip is not included in the bill.

- Tipping taxis is not customary or required.

- Tip porters US$1 per bag.

DRESS

- Appearance is quite important to Chileans, who favor sophisticated, European styles.

- It is important to be neatly and cleanly dressed for all occasions. Sloppy and tattered clothing is very unacceptable.

- Shorts are not worn in the cities but are acceptable in vacation areas.

- Wear layers; the temperature may vary greatly throughout the day. Take warmer clothes for high altitudes and evenings at the beach. Take rain gear when traveling in southern Chile.

BUSINESS

- Men: Conservative, dark suits. Men should wear jackets regardless of where they are or how hot it is.

- Women: Dresses and suits. Nylons are not necessary in the summer. Bare legs are acceptable with dresses.

EVENING/ENTERTAINMENT

- Men: Suits and ties.

- Women: Elegant, tasteful clothing. Chilean women do not favor overtly sexy clothing.

CASUAL

- Men and women: Pants or designer jeans.

- Expensive, flashy gifts may cause awkwardness. Tastes are conservative.

- Open gifts immediately in front of the giver.

HOSTESS

- Bring a bouquet of flowers to the hostess, or send flowers in advance of a party.

- Give flowers, wine, chocolates, local crafts from your home, small porcelain pieces or an art object to hang on a wall.

- It is nice to bring a gift for the children.

BUSINESS

- Business gifts are not expected until a relationship is formed.

- Give leather appointment books, quality pens, cigarette lighters, office accessories, a clock or liquor.

GIFTS

It is nice to bring a gift for the children.

HELPFUL HINTS

- There are change houses (*casas de cambio*) available for exchanging currency. They are generally easier to find than banks, and the rates are the same.

- Cash machines are common in bigger cities.

- Chilean phone systems are better than in the rest of South America.

- The postal system is efficient.

To understand Chile, read Isabel Allende's House of the Spirits *or* Love and Shadows.

DO

- Bring plenty of film if you will be taking pictures. Film may be expensive or hard to find.

- Bargain in street markets.

- To understand Chile, read Isabel Allende's *House of the Spirits* or *Love and Shadows*. Allende is one of Chile's best and most popular writers.

DO NOT

- Do not try to bribe anyone, especially not the police.

- Do not make comparisons between the United States and Chile.

- Punctuality is generally respected and expected in business. However, be prepared for Chileans to be thirty minutes late.

- Always arrive late for social functions. Being fifteen to thirty minutes late for dinner and thirty minutes late for a party is expected.

- Traffic is bad in Santiago. Plan for delays.

- Chileans don't like to feel pressured or rushed.

*Chileans don't like
to feel pressured
or rushed.*

STRICTLY BUSINESS

- Chile is a member of GATT (General Agreement on Tariffs and Trade), is waiting for NAFTA membership and is an associate member of Mercosur.

- Chileans have a positive attitude about doing business with North Americans.

CORPORATE CULTURE

- Expertise is less important than who you are—your family, your company, etc. Family and friendship play a big role in business, and whom one knows is important.

- Establish rapport first. Personal relationships are vital to doing business in Chile.

*Chileans have a
positive attitude
about doing
business with
North Americans.*

- Decision-making is centralized and decisions are made at the top level, although all levels have input. Visit top-level executives first. Mid-level executives can follow up on subsequent visits.

- Be prepared to always go through a secretary. Secretaries are screeners for their bosses.

MEETINGS

It is preferable to conduct business face to face.

- Some light conversation is customary before getting down to business.

- Present business cards to everyone in a meeting.

COMMUNICATION

- It is preferable to conduct business face to face rather than over the phone or via fax. Be prepared to take several trips to finish a business transaction.

- It is acceptable, but not yet common, to communicate via e-mail.

- Businesslike behavior with a bit of humor is appreciated. Do not attempt a hard sell approach, and avoid aggressive behavior.

- Present a well-organized plan with terms clearly defined, and financial obligations and options clearly stated.

- Chileans are straightforward about negotiations. Feelings and emotion are important in negotiation. Always get written confirmation of agreements.

- Don't expect a quick response to your e-mail, although it is acceptable to communicate this way.

Chileans are straightforward about negotiations.

BE AWARE

- The business atmosphere in Chile is more formal than in the rest of South America.

- Third party contacts are very important to business. Red tape can be considerably minimized if you have the right connections.

- Never criticize or embarrass a person in public.

Never criticize or embarrass a person in public.

- Business may be conducted more slowly than in Europe and North America.

- Stay at a top-notch hotel; you will be judged by where you stay.

ENTERTAINMENT

- Business lunches and dinners are held in restaurants, hotels or residences.

- Business lunches are popular and usually long.

APPOINTMENTS

- Appointments must be scheduled in advance. Make appointments two weeks before you arrive, then reconfirm upon arrival.

- January and February are summer holidays. Try not to schedule business appointments during this time.

BUSINESS HOURS

- Businesses open between 8:30 and 9:00 a.m. and close between 5:30 and 6:00 p.m., Monday through Friday.

- Banks are open from 9:00 a.m. to 2:00 p.m., Monday through Friday.

- Government offices are open from 9:00 a.m. to 6:00 p.m., Monday through Friday. Some are open to the public only certain hours of the day.

Traditionally, men have dominated private and public life in Chile. However, attitudes are changing at home and in the workplace. Thirty percent of the labor force are women. Many women now hold important political and business positions as ministers and top executives.

- Respect for women is traditional.

- There are strong protective laws for maternity leave, making it less desirable for employers to hire women.

- Chile is an easier place for women to do business than much of South America. However, businesswomen may still encounter a machismo ethic.

- Typical North American businesswomen are often viewed as cold, pushy and non-feminine.

- The man almost always pays the bill in a restaurant and may be embarrassed if a woman attempts to pay. This shouldn't be pressed. Don't argue. If it is important for you to pay, make arrangements in advance.

- It is common for men to stare at women. It is harmless and meant as flattery.

Many women now hold important political and business positions as ministers and top executives.

Chile is an easier place for women to do business.

HEALTH AND SAFETY

- Smog is heavy in Santiago. Take precautions if you have respiratory problems.

- Although violent crime is very low, non-violent street crime is common in Santiago and other big cities. Don't walk alone at night.

- Pickpockets and thieves are active on public transportation.

- Don't display cameras, jewelry or expensive luggage.

- Be careful swimming in the ocean—there are very strong undertows and very few lifeguards.

HOLIDAYS AND FESTIVALS

Do not plan to make a business visit or schedule any appointments during the following holidays or festivals. Be sure to check for the numerous regional and local holidays and festivals.

January	New Year's Day (1)
March/April	Good Friday (varies)
	Holy Saturday (varies)
	Easter (varies)

May	Labor Day (1)
	Naval Battle of Iquique (21)
June	Feast of St. Peter and St. Paul (29)
August	Feast of the Assumption (15)
September	Liberation Day (11)
	Independence Day (18)
	Armed Forces Day (19)
October	Columbus Day (12)
November	All Saints Day (1)
December	Immaculate Conception (8)
	Christmas (25)

23.
COLOMBIA
REPUBLIC OF COLOMBIA

VITAL STATISTICS

POPULATION: 38,300,000. More than 40 percent of the population is under the age of twenty.

CAPITAL: Bogotá, with a population of 6 million.

MAJOR CITIES: Medellín (3,000,000), Cali (2,500,000).

GEOGRAPHY: 439,735 square miles (1,139,000 square kilometers), the size of California and Texas combined. Located at the juncture of Central and South America, Colombia has an extensive coastline on both the Pacific and Atlantic Oceans. It is the only country in South America with coastline along both oceans.

GOVERNMENT: Republic, composed of 32 departments and one capital district. Presidents are elected for four-year terms and may not be re-elected to two terms in a row. The bicameral Congress consists of a 102-member Senate and a 161-member House of Representatives. Unlike many other South American countries, Colombia has had an elected government throughout most of its history. The voting age is eighteen.

ECONOMY: Colombia has one of the most successful economies in South America, despite adverse conditions and a very unequal distribution of wealth. A small number of Colombians hold most of the country's wealth and political power, but the middle and working classes are growing in Colombia's cities. Oil production is growing at a faster rate than in any other Latin American country. Agriculture plays a key role in the economy, with coffee and flowers especially important exports to the United States and Europe.

LIVING STANDARD: GDP = US$2,330 per capita.

AGRICULTURE: Coffee, bananas, flowers, cotton, sugarcane, rice, corn, tobacco, potatoes, soybeans, sorghum, plantains, cassava, cattle, sheep, port and roundwood. Colombia leads the world in production of coffee.

INDUSTRY: Foodstuffs, beverages, textiles, chemicals, machinery, vehicles, steel, metal products, tourism, mining, plastics, cardboard containers, cement, electrical products, handicrafts and light industry products.

NATURAL
RESOURCES: Coal, petroleum, natural gas, iron ore, carbon, nickel, copper, emeralds, silver, gold and fish. Colombia is the world leader in emerald mining.

CLIMATE: The climate ranges from the snow-capped peaks of the Andes mountains to tropical lowland plains. Colombia's Pacific coast has one of the highest rainfall levels in the world. Temperatures vary very little from season to season. Bogotá has an average temperature of 58°F (14°C) in January and 57°F (14°C) in July.

CURRENCY: Colombian peso. 1 peso = 100 centavos.

THE PEOPLE

CORRECT
NAME: Colombians.
                Adjective: Colombian.

ETHNIC
MAKEUP: 58 percent mestizo, 20 percent European (mostly Spanish), 14 percent mulatto, 4 percent black, 3 percent black/Native American, 1 percent Native American.

VALUE SYSTEM:	Colombians are hardworking and peace loving. Politeness, proper behavior, good manners and courtesy are valued. The individual is important. Colombians are very proud of their democracy and independence. They do not like or want outside interference and want to meet challenges on their own. Class structure and a closed political system are slowly dying, and a new appreciation for cultural and political pluralism is growing.
FAMILY:	The family is very important in Colombia. Many Colombian families are large, and several generations may live in one home. Family members share time and good fortunes. The father is the head of the household and normally provides for the family, although dual income families are on the rise. The mother is responsible for the home.
RELIGION:	95 percent Roman Catholic, 5 percent other.

Catholicism is the state religion, but freedom of religion is guaranteed. Religion is an important factor in Colombian society, although society is becoming increasingly secularized. |
| EDUCATION: | Education is free and compulsory through primary school. While the number of rural schools has increased and helped the literacy rate rise to 88 percent, fewer than 60 percent of all students complete primary education. Many wealthy |

Colombians send their children to the United States and Europe to attend colleges and universities.

SPORTS: *Fútbol* (soccer) is the most popular sport. Golf, tennis, cycling, racing, swimming, track and field, volleyball, basketball and baseball are also widely enjoyed. *Tejo*, popular in smaller towns, is a kind of "air bowling" where a stone disc is thrown toward a target.

RECREATION: Dancing, reading, sports and theater, especially North American movies with subtitles, are favorite pastimes. Bullfights are very popular. Music and dancing, including jazz, rock, salsa, merengue, cumbia (an especially beautiful dance) and pasodobles (from Spain) are popular.

IMPORTANT DATES

Pre-16th Century	Native tribes populate modern day Colombia.
1499	Alonso de Ojeda lands at Cabo de la Vela.
1500s	Spaniards settle in the region. New Granada encompasses modern day Colombia, Ecuador, Panama and Venezuela.
1810	Nationalists claim independence.
1819	Battle of Boyacá, led by Simón Bolívar, achieves Colombian independence. Gran Colombia is formed, including modern-day Colombia, Ecuador, Panama and Venezuela.

1830	Venezuela and Ecuador withdraw from Gran Colombia.
1903	Panama declares itself independent.
1948-1957	Civil war between conservatives and liberals leads to a constitutional amendment requiring the presidency to alternate between liberal and conservative parties until 1974.
1974	Free elections held.
1980s	M-19 guerrillas and Medellín and Cali drug cartels cause unrest and violence.
1990	M-19 renounces terrorism and joins the democratic process. Drug traffickers kill several presidential candidates. Despite an attempt to dissuade Colombians from voting, elections are held. César Gaviría Trujillo is elected president. Gaviría attempts to end drug violence by offering terrorist groups the right to participate in the 1991 Constitutional Convention. Drug violence diminishes.
1991	New constitution implemented, encouraging political pluralism and special rights for previously ignored Indian and black populations.
1992-1993	Drug related violence increases.
1993	Noted drug baron Pablo Escobar dies. Violence subsides.
1994	Ernesto Samper is elected president in a peaceful election.
1998	Presidential elections scheduled.

- Colombia was named for Christopher Columbus.

- Colombia, under the leadership of Simón Bolívar, was the first South American country to gain independence from Spain.

- Colombia has the greatest diversity of animal species per unit of area of any country in the world and the second greatest number of total species in the world.

- The largest emerald in the world, 632 carats, was discovered near Boyacá at the beginning of this century.

- Colombians greatly admire writers and poets.

- Colombian Gabriel García Márquez won the Nobel Prize for literature in 1982. He is considered Colombia's most outstanding modern-day writer. His tales about life in Latin America are realistic descriptions combined with fantasy.

Colombian Gabriel García Márquez won the Nobel Prize for literature in 1982.

MEETING AND GREETING

See pages 63-67.

- Shake hands with everyone when entering or leaving a room.

- Friends and family kiss one time on the right cheek. Kisses may be accompanied by a hug.

NAMES AND TITLES

See pages 69-75.

- Everyone in a high position is called "Doctor." If you are uncertain of someone's title, address him or her as "Doctor."

- Younger people use first names with each other immediately.

LANGUAGE

- The official language is Spanish.

- Colombians are very proud of their Spanish dialect, which they consider more pure than that of other South American countries.

- English and French are required courses in school. English is taught from the first year until students finish school. French is required for two years.

English is understood and used by the business community.

- English is understood and used by the business community and is spoken by many in the bigger cities. French and German are known to a lesser degree.

- The 80 different groups of ethnic Indians have 40 different languages that are used among themselves.

- Smiling is very important.

- Never put your feet on furniture in a hotel, office or home.

- Yawning is impolite and viewed as a sign of hunger or sleepiness. Always cover your mouth when yawning.

GESTURES

- Never beckon to anyone with your index finger—it is very demeaning. Beckon with your palm down, waving your fingers or your whole hand.

- Never show how tall a person is by holding out your hand with your palm facing the floor. This is used only for animals. A person's height is shown by holding your hand perpendicular to the floor.

Yawning is impolite and viewed as a sign of hunger or sleepiness.

SMALL TALK

- Talk about sports (especially soccer), coffee, art, music, culture, history, news (local if possible) and the beauty of Colombia.

- Colombians have an excellent sense of humor and love jokes, especially political and "gringo" jokes.

- Don't give your opinions about local politics or religion.

- Be prudent when you talk about drugs. Colombia is working with the United States government in the war against drugs, but U.S. foreign policy is not viewed positively by many Colombians.

Colombians have an excellent sense of humor and love jokes.

PHRASES

See page 80.

DINING AND SOCIAL EVENTS

- A small continental breakfast is typical.

- Lunch, served between 12:30 and 2:30 p.m., is the main meal.

- Supper is generally eaten around 8:00 p.m.

- Colombians are very gracious hosts. You will be offered food and drinks and made to feel welcome.

Colombians are very gracious hosts.

- Always accept coffee. Naturally, Colombians are very proud of their excellent coffee.

- Allow your hosts to seat you, and wait for the hostess to begin eating before you do.

- Never take anything to eat or drink without first offering it to others.

- To indicate you have finished eating, place your knife and fork horizontally at the 5:25 position across your plate.

- Keep your hands above the table during meals, and keep your elbows off the table.

- Never touch food on your plate with your hands.

- Your napkin should always be on your lap.

- Overeating and burping are very impolite.

- Never smack or eat with your mouth open.

- Only use a toothpick if you are alone.

- Do not eat while walking in the street.

- Colombians are becoming more sensitive about smoking in public places and in homes. Ask before you smoke.

Always accept coffee.

Rule of Thumb

Overeating and burping are very impolite.

Ask before you smoke.

FOOD

- Coffee is strong and powerful. Coffee is King!

- Colombians eat starchy foods, including potatoes, rice, noodles, stews and thick soups.

- The typical Colombian dinner always includes meat, potatoes and rice.

- Colombian seafood is wonderful.

- Sample the local rums.

- Colombians enjoy good beer. Bavaria is a popular local brand.

- A favorite dish on the coast is iguana eggs, which can be bought from street vendors.

"What's for dinner?" Meat, potatoes and rice.

TYPICAL FOODS

- *Ajiaco:* potato soup, typical in Bogotá.

- *Arroz con pollo:* chicken with rice, a popular national dish.

- *Arepa:* cornmeal pancakes.

- *Sancocho:* a meat and vegetable stew.

- *Frijoles*: red beans.

- *Agua de Panela*: a sweet drink made from sugarcane (brown sugar) dissolved in hot water. Adults and children enjoy this daily at breakfast and especially at tea time in late afternoon.

TIPPING

- A 10 percent service charge is generally included in a restaurant bill. If not, leave 10 percent on the table.

- Tip taxi drivers 10 percent.

- Tip porters US$1 bag.

- You may want to hire someone to watch your car to prevent theft. Tip this person well, or a thief might better you.

You may want to hire someone to watch your car to prevent theft.

DRESS

- Colombians pay a lot of attention to appearance and clothing. Fashionable clothing is worn in the cities.

- Dress conservatively and be well groomed.

- Shoes are the first thing people notice. Colombians do not wear tennis shoes unless they are playing tennis, jogging, etc.

- At a bullfight, dress well if you are in the expensive seats.

Colombians pay a lot of attention to appearance and clothing.

BUSINESS

- Men: Dark suits, white shirts and ties in the cities. In warmer areas, dress is less formal.

- Women: Dresses and suits. Wear comfortable cotton in warmer areas.

EVENING/ENTERTAINMENT

- Men: Sport coats or suits.

- Women: Nice cocktail dresses or dressy pants.

CASUAL

- Jeans are acceptable, if they are fashionable and clean.

GIFTS

- Gifts made in the United States will be well received.

- Give personal gifts, like clothing and perfume, only when you know people well.

HOSTESS

- Give fruit, flowers or chocolates.

- Send flowers ahead of time, if possible. Roses are a favorite flower.

BUSINESS

- Give fine scotch and wines, engraved pens, calculators and gifts from your home region.

DO

- Expect long lines and security checks of luggage at airports.

- Be prepared for long lines at government offices.

- Help women with packages.

- Be careful of your alcohol intake. Alcohol takes effect more quickly at high altitudes.

- Allow sufficient time for travel. Drivers are careless and traffic jams are common. Prepare for delays.

DO NOT

- Don't give your opinion or join in conversations about drugs unless you are extremely well-informed about the issues. Colombians are very sensitive about the problem. The vast majority are not in any way involved in drugs, and the typical Colombian has never used drugs.

Help women with packages.

Don't give your opinion or join in conversations about drugs.

- If you are invited to a bullfight, do not decline. Tickets for good seats are very expensive.

- Do not be offended if you are called a "gringo." Colombians use this term to refer to people from the United States, and it is not meant to be insulting.

- The term "mestizo" is used only for statistical purposes. Never refer to anyone as a mestizo.

- Don't change money on the street; counterfeiting is common and a serious problem.

- Colombians consider Panama stolen from them by *norteamericanos* eager to build the Panama Canal. Don't bring up this touchy subject.

PUNCTUALITY AND PACE

- Time and punctuality are not stressed.

- Colombians will typically arrive up to thirty minutes late for a social engagement. A 10:00 p.m. party will often begin half an hour to one hour late.

- In business, Colombians are normally punctual although they may be half an hour late. The best policy for foreign businesspeople is to be punctual but prepared to wait. Don't get angry if a 12:00 p.m. appointment doesn't begin until 12:30 p.m.

- Excuse yourself if you are late.

- Traffic in the cities is very bad, and everyone uses it as an excuse for lateness.

- The pace of business and negotiations may be slow.

- "In an hour or two" may mean tomorrow or next week. "Tomorrow" seldom means tomorrow and may mean next week. Don't be offended if someone says they will phone you tomorrow and then calls a week later.

- During the debt crisis of the 1980s, Colombia was the only major Latin American country that did not have to reschedule its foreign debt.

"In an hour or two" may mean tomorrow or next week.

STRICTLY BUSINESS

CORPORATE CULTURE

- Colombians want to know you personally before they do business with you. You must develop a relationship with your counterparts before they will consider you trustworthy.

MEETINGS

- Always allow your Colombian counterparts to bring up the subject of business. Be aware that this may take a while. Meetings will be slow, with quiet, deliberate discussions.

- Follow up a meeting by sending a letter summarizing the main points and what was agreed upon.

COMMUNICATION

Colombian businesspeople are formal but very gracious.

- Bring plenty of business cards.

- It is not necessary to print business cards in Spanish, but it is a nice gesture.

- It may take several trips to finish a business transaction. Colombians prefer to do business in person and you can only get so far by phone and fax.

- Colombian businesspeople are formal but very gracious.

- Maintain eye contact during conversations, or you will leave a bad impression.

- Negotiations will probably, but not necessarily, be conducted by the top person in the firm.

- Contracts will be long and detailed. Put the key aspects of agreed-to points in writing.

- Communicating by e-mail is acceptable if it is available. Do not expect an immediate response to e-mail.

- Make your presentations with flair.

Make your presentations with flair.

BE AWARE

- Always make your Colombian counterpart look good. Never embarrass anyone.

- Third party contacts are vital to your business success. You should hire a local distributor, representative, salesperson and lawyer.

- Individuality is highly valued.

Always make your Colombian counterpart look good.

ENTERTAINMENT

- Working breakfasts are common.

- Business lunches and dinners are popular. Plan on spending at least two or three hours at either.

- Colombians often entertain in their homes.

- Always reciprocate hospitality.

- Spouses will probably be invited to business dinners.

APPOINTMENTS

- Make appointments two weeks in advance of your trip, and confirm upon arrival.

BUSINESS HOURS

- Offices are generally open from 9:00 a.m. to 5:00 p.m., Monday through Friday.

- Shops are open from 9:00 a.m. to 7:00 p.m., Monday through Saturday. They may be open a few hours on Sunday.

- Banks are open from 9:00 a.m. to 3:00 p.m. and are often open an extra half hour on Fridays. On the last banking day of the month, they may close at noon.

ESPECIALLY FOR WOMEN

Colombian women have held several high-ranking jobs in the government, including Minister of Foreign Relations. Many women work outside the home, and 20 percent of the workforce are women. There are increasing numbers of Colombian women in professional and management positions.

- A woman in the workforce is treated as any man, notwithstanding special courtesy and manners.

- Colombian women like to be feminine and be treated like women. They like men to open doors, help with their coats, allow women to go first, pay the bill, light cigarettes, etc.

- United States businesswomen are received well in Colombia and will be treated in a businesslike manner, although perhaps with some curiosity. North American women should not have trouble doing business in Colombia.

- Men may flirt and make comments; simply ignore them. Women should be careful not to do anything that might be considered flirtatious, which may be misinterpreted.

Colombian women have held several high-ranking jobs in the government.

- Prepare to take a day or two to adjust to the altitude.

- Take precautions against sunburn in high-altitude areas.

- Excellent health care is available in the cities but not in rural areas.

- Drink bottled water.

- Use seat belts while in cars. It is the law.

- Before traveling to Colombia, monitor the news for several weeks concerning safety.

HEALTH AND SAFETY

Check the U.S. State Department's Travel Hotline for travel warnings.

- Your Colombian hosts will be very anxious to advise you on dangers and areas you should avoid. Heed their advice.

- Take extreme caution when traveling in Colombia. The per-capita murder rate is seven times greater than in the United States.

- Don't travel by inter-city bus. Use only official taxis from taxi stands, and when riding in a taxi, make sure all doors are locked.

- Don't accept food, drink or cigarettes from strangers.

- Be careful of pickpockets. Don't show your valuables on the street.

- Colombians don't pay by credit card on the phone or by computer, for fear of their numbers being stolen and used. Exercise caution in this regard.

Do not plan to make a business visit or schedule any appointments during the following holidays or festivals. Be sure to check for the numerous regional and local holidays and festivals.

January	New Year's Day (1)
	Epiphany (6)*
March	St. Joseph's Day (19)*
March/April	Holy Thursday (varies)
	Good Friday (varies)
	Easter (varies)
May	Labor Day (1)
	Feast of the Ascension (varies)
June	Corpus Christi (varies)
	Sacred Heart of Jesus (varies)
July	Feast of St. Peter and St. Paul (1)
	Independence Day (20)
August	Battle of Boyacá (7)
	Feast of the Assumption (15)*
October	Columbus Day (Día de la Raza) (12)*
November	All Saints' Day (1)
	Independence of Cartagena (11)*
December	Immaculate Conception (8)
	Christmas (25)

*celebrated the following Monday

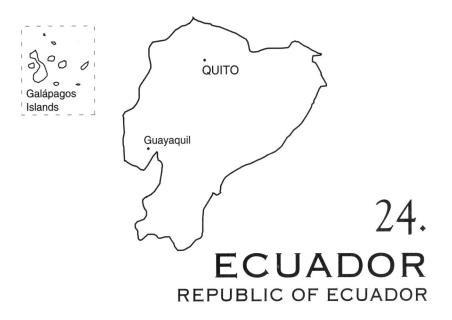

Galápagos
Islands

QUITO

Guayaquil

24.

ECUADOR
REPUBLIC OF ECUADOR

VITAL STATISTICS

POPULATION: 10,891,000.

CAPITAL: Quito, with a population of 1,101,000. Quito is
                one of the oldest continuously inhabited cities in
                the Western Hemisphere.

MAJOR CITIES: Guayaquil (1.7 million), the largest city in
                Ecuador.

GEOGRAPHY: 109,483 square miles (284,560 square
                kilometers), slightly smaller than Nevada. There
                are four major geographical regions: *La Costa*, a
                coastal plain that has rich agricultural land; *La
                Sierra*, a highland region with snow-capped
                volcanoes and mountains; *La Amazonia*, the
                Amazon basin, a tropical rain forest; and

Archipiélago de Colón or the Galápagos Islands, a group of islands in the Pacific Ocean about 600 miles off the coast.

GOVERNMENT: Republic, composed of 21 provinces. The president is the head of the executive branch and cannot run for re-election. The unicameral legislature, the National Congress, has 77 seats. Legislators must sit out a term before running again. Citizens over the age of eighteen have the right to vote, and voting is compulsory for those who are literate.

ECONOMY: Government policies encouraging foreign investment, trade and free markets have led to increased opportunity for all Ecuadorians. However, economic growth has been uneven in recent years due to fluctuations in prices for Ecuador's primary exports, oil and bananas. Ecuador is the second largest producer of oil in South America. In 1992, Ecuador resigned from OPEC, protesting that the cartel doesn't benefit smaller oil producers.

LIVING
STANDARD: GDP = US$4,350 per capita.

AGRICULTURE: Bananas, coffee, sugarcane, rice, palm products, corn, potatoes, cacao, pork, cattle, sheep, chickens and roundwood.

INDUSTRY:	Foodstuffs, beverages, petroleum products, textile products, pharmaceuticals, lumber, chemicals, food processing, fishing and timber.

NATURAL
RESOURCES: Petroleum, fish, shrimp, timber, gold and limestone. Petroleum and petroleum products account for two-thirds of the nation's exports.

CLIMATE: Varies with altitude. The coastal lowlands are hot and humid. The highlands consist of subtropical valleys and frigid mountains. The rainy season is from November to May throughout the country.

CURRENCY: Sucre. 1 sucre = 100 centavos.

THE PEOPLE

CORRECT
NAME: Ecuadorians.
Adjective: Ecuadorian.

ETHNIC
MAKEUP: 55 percent mestizo, 25 percent Native American, 10 percent European, 3 percent black, 7 percent other.

VALUE SYSTEM: Ecuadorians are hospitable and warmly welcoming of visitors. They revere older people and honor experience and authority. Superiors, parents and teachers are greatly respected. It is unheard of for a child to be impolite to a teacher. Ecuador is one of the most racially divided countries of South America. Whites (*Blancos*) are better off economically and educationally than the rest of the population. Mestizos are usually middle class. Native Ecuadorians (*Indios*) are considered lower class, and many live in poverty, are illiterate and often don't speak Spanish. Blacks have overcome many stereotypes. Miss Ecuador, 95-96, Monica Chala, was an Afro-Ecuadorian.

FAMILY:

Families are very important, and many generations may live together. Great respect is shown for the elderly, and their opinions are valued. Families are getting smaller. Women typically marry by age twenty (fourteen in some rural areas). Men usually marry around age 23.

RELIGION:

95 percent Roman Catholic, 5 percent other.

The Catholic Church has a strong influence on personal and social behavior. Many official holidays come from the Catholic faith. Freedom of religion is guaranteed, and people are tolerant of other beliefs.

EDUCATION:

School is mandatory from ages six to fourteen. Both private and public schools offer a good education. The literacy rate is 87 percent.

SPORTS:	*Fútbol* (soccer) is the favorite sport. Volleyball, track, tennis, basketball and boxing are also widely enjoyed. *Pelota nacional* is a popular sport, similar to racquetball, in which two people use small paddles and a small ball against a backboard.
RECREATION:	The merengue and salsa are popular dances. North American and Latin music are popular. The Quito Symphony is excellent, and folk dance companies and amateur theater are popular with all. Ecuadorians are great supporters of the arts, and Quito boasts several wonderful museums. In the 17th and 18th centuries, Quito became famous as an art center. Architecture, sculpture and paintings from that period are considered the finest examples of Spanish art.

IMPORTANT DATES

Pre-16th Century	Quitos and Caras, advanced tribes with ancient cultures, flourish in the area. The Incas conquer them in the late 15th century.
1534	Ruminahui, the last Incan general, burns Quito to the ground to keep it from being taken by the Spanish. The Spanish take control of Ecuador.
1822	Antonio José de Sucre, a compatriot of Simón Bolívar, defeats the Spanish in the Battle of Pichinacha. Ecuador gains independence as part of Gran Colombia (Greater Colombia).

1830	Ecuador becomes a separate republic.
1830-1948	Ecuador's unstable government changes hands 62 times.
1925	Isidro Ayora modernizes the economic system in Ecuador.
1941	Peru and Ecuador battle for control of an area rich in mineral wealth in the southern Amazon region.
1942	A treaty, the Rio de Janeiro Protocol, mediated by Argentina, Brazil, Chile and the United States, gives Peru most of the disputed territory. Ecuador rejects this treaty.
1948	Galo Plaza Lasso becomes the first freely elected leader to serve a full term. Two peaceful administrations follow.
1963-1979	Military rule alternates with civilian governments.
1979	A new constitution takes effect. President Jaime Roldos is elected in a free election.
1981	President Roldos dies in a plane crash. New governmental stability is upheld with the peaceful succession of his vice president.
1992	Fourth consecutive peaceful transition of power and renewed commitment to democratic rule.
1996	Abdala Bucaram elected President with his party holding only 19 of 82 legislative seats.
1997	Bucaram ousted amid charges of corruption. Fabian Alarcón becomes interim president.
1998	Although the next presidential elections are not scheduled until 2000, elections may be held in 1998 because an interim president is currently holding the office.

- Ecuador is named after the equator.

- The Sun Museum in San Antonio borders the equator. One entrance reads "Southern Hemisphere," and the other reads "Northern Hemisphere."

- The Galápagos Islands, made famous by Charles Darwin's writings, are part of Ecuador. Galápagos, loosely translated, means "Island of the Tortoise."

- In the remote southeastern town of Vilcabamba, people reputedly live longer than anywhere else in the world. Many inhabitants have lived to be over one hundred years old.

See pages 63-67.

- People shake hands when meeting for the first time.

- Men may embrace each other if they are good friends.

- Ecuadorians kiss once when they meet friends. They do not kiss in business when meeting for the first time.

NAMES AND TITLES	See pages 69-75. • People are addressed by a title: Señor, Señora, Doctor, Doctora. First names are not used until a friendship is formed. • Don and Doña followed by a first name are used to show respect for older, famous or highly regarded people.
LANGUAGE	• Spanish is the official language. • Quechua, a combination of many dialects, is the most widely used Indian language. While only spoken by 7 percent of the population, it is recognized by the constitution as an important part of the culture. Many Quechua words have been adopted into the language and have replaced Spanish words. • English is understood by many in business.
BODY LANGUAGE	• There is a good deal of touching among friends and family. • Ecuadorians use their hands to emphasize or replace verbal communication. • Yawning in public is rude.

- Fidgeting with hands and feet is distracting and considered impolite.

- It is rude to whistle at people to get their attention.

GESTURES

- To indicate "I'll be back," Ecuadorians draw a circle in the air with an index finger.

- Holding out a hand, as though to shake hands, and twisting it back and forth means "no."

- It is impolite to point at someone. Ecuadorians may point by puckering or pursing their lips.

- An Ecuadorian may show directions by lifting or lowering his or her chin.

Faux Pas

It is impolite to point at someone.

- Ecuadorians will discuss any topic but they don't change their minds easily.

- Talk about family, history and culture.

- Show interest and curiosity about Ecuador.

- People are very interested in and enjoy discussing government and politics.

SMALL TALK

Show interest and curiosity about Ecuador.

- Don't talk about the United States' political influence, Ecuador's poverty or relations with Peru. Avoid discussing topics that imply another country's superiority.

PHRASES

See page 80.

DINING AND SOCIAL EVENTS

- Lunch is the main meal.

- All holidays are associated with a certain type of food. Every town has its own specialty dish.

- Drinks and appetizers may start at 8:00 p.m. Dinner may not be served until 11:00 p.m. or midnight. Be prepared to make a night of it. A party may not end until 4:00 or 5:00 a.m. Sometimes breakfast is served before the last guests leave.

- There is no such thing as a party without dancing. Ecuadorians learn to dance at the same time they learn to walk.

- Being invited to someone's home for a visit is a sign of friendship and should be viewed as a great honor.

There is no such thing as a party without dancing.

- The host and hostess sit at opposite ends of the table. The guest of honor is seated to the right of the hostess.

- Allow your host to make the first toast.

- Ecuadorians enjoy meal times, and conversation is lively. Dinners are considered social events, and business should not be discussed. Stay for conversation after the meal is finished. It is impolite to leave right away.

Make sure to thank the hostess.

- When guests are invited to a restaurant, the host pays for the meal.

- It is rude to call for a waiter by clapping your hands over your head, but some people do it. It is better to simply put up your index finger.

FOOD

- Soup is almost always served at midday and again at the evening meal.

Hot bread is a popular afternoon snack.

- Hot bread is a popular afternoon snack.

- Ecuadorians serve wonderful banana dishes.

- Ecuador produces excellent beer.

- Most alcohol is imported and very expensive.

TYPICAL FOODS

- *Cuy:* roasted guinea pig, very popular in the Highlands.

- *Mondongo soup:* a soup made with hominy.

- *Llapingachos:* potato and cheese pancakes.

- *Empañadas:* pastries filled with meat or cheese.

- *Locro:* a stew with potatoes, cheese and avocados (sometimes also with meat).

- *Humitas:* a sweet corn tamale.

- *Ceviche:* seafood marinated in lime with cilantro, onions, tomatoes and hot peppers.

- *Arroz con pollo:* boiled chicken with rice and spices.

- *Fritada:* pork that is boiled and then fried in its own grease.

- *Arroz con menestra:* rice with spicy beans, barbecued beef and refried bananas.

- *Caldo de bola:* a banana-based soup with meat and vegetables.

- *Hornado:* slow cooked pork.

Ecuadorians serve wonderful banana dishes.

TIPPING

- In restaurants, 20 percent is added to the check. Ten percent goes to the state for sales tax, and 10 percent goes to the business. If no service charge is included on a restaurant bill, tip 10 percent. If a service charge is included, you may leave a small additional tip for good service.

- It is not necessary to tip taxis.

- Tip porters US$1 per bag.

DRESS

- Styles are European and conservative.

- Dress is more casual in coastal areas, where the climate is hot and humid.

BUSINESS

- Men: Suits and ties for formal meetings. Light shirts may be worn to casual business or business/social meetings.

- Women: Suits for a first meeting. After that, comfortable dresses.

Dress is more casual in coastal areas.

EVENING/ENTERTAINMENT

- Men: Dark suits, jackets and ties.

- Women: Dresses and cocktail dresses.

CASUAL

- Modest shorts may be worn in recreational areas. Shorts are not worn in the cities.

GIFTS

- Name brands are appreciated.

- Levi and Guess jeans are very expensive and very popular.

- Be very demonstrative in your thanks when you are given a gift.

- After dinner, hosts may give the guests a small gift.

HOSTESS

- If invited to a home for a meal, send or bring flowers. Send a thank-you note afterwards.

- Give flowers, pastries, chocolates, wine, liquors or items for the home.

- Do not give lilies or marigolds, which are considered funeral flowers.

- A gift for the children is appreciated. North American candy bars are popular—Milky Ways, Snickers, etc.

Hot Wheels and Barbies are excellent gifts for children.

BUSINESS

- Business gifts are exchanged after negotiations are over.

- Give desk accessories or pictures and books, especially about your region or country.

- What we call "going Dutch" (splitting the bill), Ecuadorians call "doing as the North Americans."

- Gas is very expensive, which is ironic, since it is one of Ecuador's main exports.

DO

- Use your credit cards. Upper-class people use credit cards for absolutely everything.

- Bring your own film, as it is very expensive.

- Ask for permission before photographing Indians.

DO NOT

- Ecuadorians hate to be stereotyped. Recognize their uniqueness.

- Never change money on the street.

- Don't talk about Peru. Relations have always been strained.

HELPFUL HINTS

U.S. money, especially large bills, may not be accepted due to counterfeiting problems.

PUNCTUALITY AND PACE

- Ecuadorians are not punctual. Arriving fifteen to twenty minutes late is considered "on time."

- All foreigners should be punctual for business meetings.

- Guests are not expected to arrive on time for a social event. Arrive half an hour to an hour late for a party.

STRICTLY BUSINESS

CORPORATE CULTURE

- The individual is more important than the group. Identity comes from the position and history of your extended family.

- Family and friends play a major role in business associations.

- The "old boy" network is very important.

- Superiors are treated in a friendly but always respectful manner.

Identity comes from the position and history of your extended family.

MEETINGS

- Business meetings are held in offices or restaurants.

- Meetings will probably start later than the scheduled time.

- Meetings start with small talk before business discussions begin.

COMMUNICATION

- Business cards should be printed in both English and Spanish.

- Your title and academic degrees should be on your business cards.

- Communicating by fax is very common in business, and e-mail is becoming more common. Do not expect e-mail to be responded to quickly.

- Ecuadorians negotiate with people, not companies. Never change your negotiating team. Be prepared to take several trips to conduct a business transaction.

- Negotiations can be lengthy. Be patient and expect delays.

- Private business people may speak English, but few government officials will. You will need to hire an interpreter.

BE AWARE

- Hire a local contact—a business consultant or lawyer—when doing business in Ecuador.

- Business relations are more formal in the highlands than on the coast.

ENTERTAINMENT

- Business lunches are common.

- Many executives don't arrive at the office until after 10:00 a.m. Many business people start the day by playing tennis or golf at their club, then taking a Turkish bath and having breakfast before going into their office. A great deal of business gets done this way.

APPOINTMENTS

- Set up your appointments at least two weeks before going to Ecuador. Very few businesses schedule appointments a day in advance.

BUSINESS HOURS

- Offices are generally open Monday through Friday from 8:00 a.m. to 6:00 p.m., with a two hour lunch period from noon to 2:00 p.m.

- In the warm, humid coastal region, the lunch period may last two and a half to three hours.

- Banks are open from 9:00 a.m. to 1:30 p.m., Monday through Friday. After-hour services

Many business people start the day by playing tennis or golf at their club, then taking a Turkish bath and having breakfast before going into their office.

may be offered until 6:00 p.m. during the week and from 9:00 a.m. to 1:00 p.m. on Saturdays.

Machismo is still the model for men. Men are heads of households, and women are the managers. Opportunities for and attitudes toward women are changing rapidly in Ecuador. More and more women are working and holding leadership positions in business and, especially, in the government. The vice president of Ecuador elected in 1996 was a woman.

- Foreign women should have no problems doing business in Ecuador.

- Men will expect to pay the bill at a restaurant. It is polite for a woman to offer, but she will be refused. Arrange to pay ahead of time if it is important for you to pay.

- Ecuadorians are not accustomed to seeing women drink whiskey or hard liquor. Women drink wine.

- Arrive a day early to adjust to Quito's high altitude.

- Drink bottled water and peel raw vegetables and fruits.

ESPECIALLY FOR WOMEN

Women drink wine.

HEALTH AND SAFETY

- Quito has a smog problem.

- Street crime is very high in Quito and Guayaquil. Avoid walking downtown alone. Whenever possible, see the cities with Ecuadorian colleagues.

- Banditry is common in mountain regions, especially around Quito. When traveling, have a qualified guide and travel in groups of four or more.

- Avoid the regions bordering Colombia and Peru.

HOLIDAYS AND FESTIVALS

- Do not plan to make a business visit or schedule any appointments during the following holidays or festivals. Be sure to check for the numerous regional and local holidays and festivals.

January	New Year's Day (1)
February/March	Carnival (the three days before Ash Wednesday, varies)
March/April	Holy Thursday (varies)
	Good Friday (varies)
	Easter (varies)
May	Labor Day (1)
	Battle of Pichincha Day (24)

June	Corpus Christi (varies)
July	Bolívar's Birthday (24)
	Founding of Guayaquil (25)
August	Independence Day (10)
October	Guayaquil's Independence Day (9)
	Columbus Day (12)
November	All Saints' Day (1)
	Memorial Day (2)
	Cuenca's Independence Day (3)
December	Quito Foundation Day (6)
	Feast of the Immaculate Conception (8)
	Christmas (25)

- Carnival is a major event in Ecuador, as in most other South American countries. Celebrating begins as early as January and reaches a climax on Ash Wednesday. Every city has its own special celebration. Part of the fun and festivities is throwing water and water balloons at passers-by: be prepared to get wet!

Put Your Best Foot Forward

Filadelfia •

Concepción •

ASUNCIÓN
•

Ciudad •
del Este

25.

PARAGUAY
REPUBLIC OF PARAGUAY

VITAL STATISTICS

POPULATION: 5.3 million. Forty percent of the population is under the age of fifteen.

CAPITAL: Asunción, with a population of 800,000.

MAJOR CITIES: Ciudad del Este (50,000).

GEOGRAPHY: 157,047 square miles (406,750 square kilometers), slightly smaller than California. Paraguay is landlocked, but the Paraná River leads to the sea. The Paraguay River divides the nation into the northwest—*Gran Chaco*—an arid, desolate area; and the southeast, which consists of fertile, grassy farmland leading into hilly, forested country.

GOVERNMENT:	Republic, composed of 17 departments. The president is chief of state and head of government. The bicameral Congress consists of a 45-seat Chamber of Senators and 80-seat Chamber of Deputies. All citizens between the ages of 18 and 60 are required to vote.
ECONOMY:	Inflation, foreign debt and high unemployment plague this young democracy. Paraguay has joined the Mercosur trade agreement in an effort to strengthen its economic activity. There is a large gap between the rich and poor. A few elite families control nearly all the resources, and economic opportunities are limited to urban dwellers.
LIVING STANDARD:	GDP = US$1,621 per capita. The GDP has doubled in the last generation.
AGRICULTURE:	Cotton, beef, corn, sugarcane, soybeans, tobacco and lumber. Paraguay is the world's largest producer of soybeans.
INDUSTRY:	Cement, textiles, beverages and wood products.
NATURAL RESOURCES:	Hydroelectric sites and forests. More than one-third of the country is forest, but deforestation has damaged potential for the timber industry.
CLIMATE:	Temperate to subtropical southeast of the Paraguay River, semiarid to the northwest.
CURRENCY:	Guaraní. 1 guaraní = 100 centimos.

THE PEOPLE

CORRECT
NAME: Paraguayans.
                     Adjective: Paraguayan.

ETHNIC
MAKEUP: 95 percent mestizo, 5 percent Native American.
                     Paraguay is the most homogeneous nation in
                     South America.

VALUE
SYSTEM: Paraguayans are traditional, conservative people
                     who strive for tranquillity (tranquilidad).
                     Paraguay has historically been voluntarily
                     isolated. In the 19th century, the government
                     tried to seal the borders in an attempt to become
                     self-sufficient. More recently, very strict
                     government controls have isolated the people
                     from most outside information. Paraguayans
                     have called their landlocked country "an island
                     surrounded by land."

FAMILY: The extended family is the cornerstone of the
                     society. People gain stability and security from
                     their family. Three generations often live
                     together, and people expect to care for their aged
                     parents. A person's family determines his or her
                     position in society. Study and preparation are
                     necessary to go into the professions, but a
                     person's last name is still more influential than
                     any other factor.

RELIGION:	96 percent Catholic, 4 percent other.
	Catholicism is the official religion. The state pays church salaries and makes all church appointments. Religious freedom is guaranteed. There are communities of Mennonites and some other Protestant denominations. Elements of mystical powers persist in rural worship.
EDUCATION:	Public education is free. While most children begin school, fewer than 40 percent complete six years of primary school. There is little incentive for students to finish school, since opportunities for jobs are limited. The literacy rate is officially 90 percent, but this reflects only the urban population. It is probably lower for the entire country.
SPORTS:	Paraguayans are great sports fans. Soccer (*fútbol*) is the most popular spectator sport, and volleyball is the most popular participation sport. Basketball and horse racing are also popular.
RECREATION:	Visiting family and friends is enjoyed by all. People in the cities attend plays and movies. Asunción boasts excellent theaters, museums and art galleries. The Guaranía, a slow-paced music, and the polka are traditional music forms. The Paraguayan harp is world famous.

IMPORTANT DATES

Pre-16th Century	Guaraní Indians populate modern day Paraguay.
1524	Spanish explorers arrive.
1527	Sebastián Cabot visits the area.
1537	Asunción is founded by Juan de Salazár.
1811	Paraguay overthrows local Spanish authority and gains independence.
1814-1840	José Gaspar Rodriguez de Francia rules in the first of a long line of Paraguayan dictatorships.
1865-1870	War of the Triple Alliance against Brazil, Argentina and Uruguay. 500,000 Paraguayans die, including nearly every male over age twelve. Foreign troops occupy the nation until 1896.
1932-1935	Chaco War. Paraguay acquires all the territory north of Filadelfia from Bolivia, costing the loss of a great deal of the male population.
1954	General Alfredo Stroessner, commander of the army, takes power and is reelected through 1988. Stroessner became the longest-serving dictator in the Western Hemisphere.
1989	Stroessner ousted in military coup headed by General Andrés Rodríguez Pedotti.
1991	A multi-party constituent assembly drafts a new constitution.
June 1992	New constitution goes into effect, thus establishing a democratic system of government.
May 1993	Colorado Party candidate Juan Carlos Wasmosy Monti, a civilian, is elected president.
April 1996	Army chief General Lino Oviedo attempts a coup, but popular commitment to democracy prevents a military takeover.
1998	Presidential elections are scheduled.

PARAGUAYAN FACTS

- Pre-Columbian cave art and writing can be found in some rural areas.

- The Guayaki Indians have such light skin and hair that they are called "White Indians." Their origins are a mystery.

- Agustín Barrios, "Mengoré," (1885-1944) was a famous Paraguayan musician. His compositions, such as "La Paraguay," were inspired by his homeland.

- The Itaipu Dam, a joint engineering project between Paraguay and Brazil, is the world's largest hydroelectric dam. Tours are available.

MEETING AND GREETING

See pages 63-67.

- Men and women always shake hands when greeting, even if they have met earlier in the day.

- Paraguayans kiss twice when meeting friends and family members.

NAMES AND TITLES

See pages 69-75.

- Everyone in Paraguay has two first names. It is very unusual for a person to have only one first name.

- Older people are formal about the use of names and titles. Younger people are more casual and may use first names immediately.

- Lawyers are always called "Doctor."

- In rural areas, people often address each other by their first names, preceding men's names with "Karai" and women's names with "Ña."

LANGUAGE

- Spanish and Guaraní are the official languages. Paraguayans say that Spanish is the language of the head and Guaraní is the language of the heart.

- Ninety percent of Paraguayans speak Guaraní, and 75 percent speak Spanish.

- Most people speak a mixture of Spanish and Guaraní, called *"jopará."*

- All business people speak Spanish. Castellano Spanish, the dialect of Castile, is spoken rather than español.

- Be aware that some Spanish words have different meanings in Paraguay. For example, the verb *"coger"* means "to catch" in many countries, but in Paraguay, it means "to fornicate."

- Portuguese is often spoken close to the Brazilian border.

- Many business executives will speak English.

BODY LANGUAGE

- Paraguayans are polite and soft-spoken. They do not appreciate shouting or rude behavior. Exhibit patience in all of your actions.

- Good posture is important. Try to keep your feet on the floor, and never prop them up on a piece of furniture.

- Never enter the yard of a home uninvited.

GESTURES

- The "thumbs-up" gesture is used to signify anything positive or encouraging.

- Wagging the index finger indicates "no" or "I don't think so."

- A chin flick (rubbing your hand under your chin) means "I don't know."

- Kissing fingertips means "beautiful" and is used for everything, from a person, to a wine, to a car, to a soccer play.

- Talk about family, sports, current events, weather and the Paraguayan harp.

- Ask about the Guaraní language.

- Paraguayans are very proud of their country and will appreciate your interest in it.

- Don't give your opinion about local politics.

- Don't refer to yourself as an American. Refer to yourself as a North American or as a citizen of the United States.

Paraguayans are very proud of their country and will appreciate your interest in it.

PHRASES

See page 80 for Spanish phrases.

Learn a few words and phrases in Guaraní:

English	Guaraní	Pronunciation
How are you?	*Mba'ei chapa*	mbah ASHA-pah
Hello, how is it going, my friend?	*Mba'eiko chera'a*	MBAH-akou shey-RAH-ah
I'm fine	*Iporã*	EE-por-ar
I'm happy	*Che retiae*	shay ray-tee-AH-ay
Pretty woman	*Cuñatai porá*	koo-NYAH-tah-eh POH-ra
I love you	*Rohiyju*	roh-HI-huh

DINING AND SOCIAL EVENTS

- Lunch is the main meal of the day. Businesspeople and schoolchildren go home at noon to have lunch with their family. It may be followed by an hour-long nap before everyone returns to work and school.

- Tea *(merienda)* is served around 5:00 p.m. "to fool your stomach to last until dinner at 10:00 p.m."

- Dinner is usually served around 10:00 p.m. and never earlier than 9:00 p.m. Never invite anyone for a 7:00 p.m. dinner, which would be far too early. Invite people at 8:30 or 9:00 p.m., and serve dinner at 10:00 p.m.

- When dining continental style, it is customary to hold your fork constantly in your left hand.

- Don't put your hands in your lap while eating. Rest your wrists, but never your elbows, lightly on the table.

- Guests are served full plates of food. Show that you enjoy your food. Eat dinner and accept seconds, which will probably be pressed upon you. Not finishing all the food offered is a compliment to your host.

- Paraguayans share. They buy rounds of drinks and offer food to all.

- Paraguayans visit unannounced and often. Visitors are welcomed graciously and offered food and drinks. People like meeting new people and hosting friends.

FOOD

- Paraguay is a major cattle producer. Beef is very cheap and is often eaten twice a day.

- A staple of the Paraguayan diet and culture is *cássava (mandioca)*, eaten at almost every meal. *Cássava* is a starch root vegetable that can be boiled or ground into flour and made into *chipá*, a bread.

- Paraguayans don't eat a lot of vegetables.

TYPICAL FOODS

- *Asado*: barbecued beef.

Paraguay is a major cattle producer.

- *Maté*: a hot tea made from leaves of a holly tree, *yerba maté*. Served cold, it is called *tereré* and is the national drink. Enjoy this delicious beverage, which is served everywhere.

- *Cocido*: a tea-like drink.

- *Mandioca Sopa Paraguaya*: not a soup, but thin, round cornbread baked with Paraguayan cheese, filled with eggs, cheese, ham or beef, and closed like a semi-circular pie.

- *Tortillas*: made with flour, milk, eggs and rice—thick, like pancakes.

- *Empañadas*: deep-fried meat or vegetable pockets.

- *Puchero*: meat cooked with vegetables.

TIPPING

- Tips are generally not expected.

- Tip 10 percent at a restaurant if a service charge is not included.

- Do not tip taxi drivers.

- Tip porters US$1 per bag.

DRESS

- Paraguayans dress conservatively.

- North American fashions are popular.

- Hair, nails, makeup, and dress are all important, regardless of a person's economic condition. Even the poorest people are well-groomed and clean. Beauty is important for all classes.

- Women in the major cities dress stylishly and consider appearance very important.

- The weather is hot and humid in the summer. Wear cotton. Women do not wear nylons in the summer.

- Bring a sweater during the winter months. While weather seldom gets cold, central heating in buildings may not be very effective.

- Be prepared for sudden changes in the weather.

Bring a sweater during the winter months.

BUSINESS

- Men: Dark suits and ties for initial meetings. Follow your Paraguayan counterparts' lead in dressing after the first visit.

- Women: Suits and dresses.

EVENING/ENTERTAINMENT

- Men: Dark suits and ties.

- Women: Dresses, cocktail dresses and dressy pants.

CASUAL

- Jeans are worn everywhere.

- Do not wear shorts.

GIFTS

- Give high quality gifts.

- Gifts from your country and home region will be appreciated.

- Sweets (cookies and candies) from Argentina are delicious and prized by Paraguayans.

- Giving a knife suggests "cutting off" the relationship. The "cutting" can be blunted by including a coin with the knife. This is an old tradition.

HOSTESS

- Give flowers and chocolates.

- Gifts for children are appreciated.

Barbie dolls and Power Rangers are popular with young children.

BUSINESS

- Give pens and gifts from your home region.

- If you are giving a gift with your company logo, it should be discreetly displayed.

DO

- Men offer their seats to women, especially if they are older or have babies.

- Visit a barbecue and steak restaurant featuring local entertainment.

Do not photograph anything associated with the military.

DO NOT

- Do not photograph anything associated with the military, including soldiers, bridges or equipment.

- The term "mestizo" is only used in stating statistics. People are not called mestizos.

- Paraguayans may be late, but visitors are expected to be punctual for business meetings.

- Business appointments often begin ten to twenty minutes late.

- An 8:00 p.m. social engagement could begin at 9:00 or 9:30 p.m.

CORPORATE CULTURE

- Connections are more important than expertise. Personal relationships are more important than business relationships.

MEETINGS

- Meetings rarely start on time.

- Take time to make "small talk" with colleagues before the meeting begins.

- Negotiating and decision making will probably proceed slowly. Be patient.

COMMUNICATION

- You do not need to print materials in Guaraní.

- In-person communication is vital to doing business in Paraguay. You will only be able to go so far communicating by phone or fax.

- It is acceptable to e-mail a business associate. Do not expect a quick response.

BE AWARE

- Hire a local contact to represent you in the Paraguayan business community.

- Send the same company representative to negotiate deals. A new person will need to start from scratch.

ENTERTAINMENT

- Business lunches have not been common in the past because most Paraguayans go home at noon to lunch with their families. The business lunch is becoming more popular.

Rule of Thumb

Take time to make "small talk" with colleagues before the meeting begins.

Hire a local contact to represent you.

- Dinner is a social event. Do not talk business unless your host initiates it.

APPOINTMENTS

- Make appointments at least two weeks and as much as one month in advance.

- Avoid the summer months, especially January and February, for business trips. Many offices are closed during this vacation period.

BUSINESS HOURS

- Offices are generally open from 8:00 a.m. to noon and 3:00 p.m. to 6:00 p.m., Monday through Friday, and from 8:00 a.m. to noon on Saturdays.

- Banking hours are from 8:45 a.m. to 4:00 p.m. Monday through Friday.

- June through October is the best time to do business.

- Avoid the two weeks preceding Christmas and Easter, Carnival week (the week before Ash Wednesday) and Independence Day week (in May).

Dinner is a social event.

December through February is summer vacation time.

ESPECIALLY FOR WOMEN

Women have held a very important place in Paraguayan history, due in part to the great loss of men during the War of the Triple Alliance and the Chaco War. Presently, up to 40 percent of the urban workforce is composed of women. Many women are doctors and lawyers and hold positions in banks and government offices.

- Divorce was only recently legalized. Single mothers are now working mothers, and legal and societal reforms are following this trend.

- Machismo is strong, but women are respected. Men will go out of their way to avoid confronting or offending a woman.

- By law, men are the administers of goods for the family, but in reality the women "wear the pants."

HEALTH AND SAFETY

- Water is not always safe to drink, especially outside the urban areas.

- The crime rate is high in the cities, especially near hotels and airports and after dark.

- The U.S. Federal Aviation Administration suggests that travelers limit or avoid flights within the country. Paraguay's safety standards do not meet minimum international requirements.

- Pack all valuables in your carry-on luggage. Checked luggage may be pilfered.

HOLIDAYS AND FESTIVALS

Do not plan to make a business visit or schedule any appointments during the following holidays or festivals. Be sure to check for the numerous regional and local holidays and festivals.

January	New Year's Day (1)
	Epiphany (6)
February	San Blás, Asunción's patron saint (3)
February/March	Carnival (the week before Ash Wednesday)
March	Heroes' Day (1)
March/April	Holy Week (the week before Easter)
May	Labor Day (1)
	Independence Day (14-15)
June	Chaco Armistice (12)
August	Founding of Asunción (15)
	Constitution Day (25)
September	Victory of Baquerón (29)
October	Columbus Day (12)
November	All Saints Day (1)
	Immaculate Conception (8)
December	Christmas (25)

Holy Week (Semana Santa) is a very important holiday time and a week for family gatherings.

Iquitos •

• Piura

• Trujillo

• LIMA
Callao •
• Ica
Cuzco •
Arequipa •

26.
PERU
REPUBLIC OF PERU

VITAL STATISTICS

POPULATION: 23,500,000. Half the population is under age twenty.

CAPITAL: Lima, with a population of 6,054,000.

MAJOR CITIES: Arequipa (939,000), Callao (560,000), Trujillo (491,000).

GEOGRAPHY: 496,222 square miles (1,285,220 square kilometers), about the size of Alaska. Peru is the third largest country in South America. Three distinct regions exist in Peru: *Costa*—the narrow, dry coastal plain along the Pacific Ocean where the majority of the population lives; *Sierra*—the high Andes mountains in the center of Peru; and *Selva*—the tropical lowlands of the Amazon Basin in the east. The Amazonian jungle covers sixty percent of Peru.

GOVERNMENT: Republic, divided into 24 departments and one constitutional province. The president is the chief of state and head of government. The unicameral Congress has 120 seats. All citizens over age eighteen may vote.

ECONOMY: The Peruvian economy has faced severe strains. In 1990, inflation rose to over 7,600 percent while wages fell. Peru is the world's largest producer of coca leaf and drug trade is a major obstacle to economic growth.

Peru has now committed to a free market economy and increased foreign investment is stimulating economic growth and creating new jobs. Living conditions, while still poor, are expected to improve in the next few years. With untapped resources, an educated workforce and a more fair distribution of income than many other South American countries, the future looks brighter, and Peruvians are generally optimistic. In 1994, the economy grew 12.9 percent, one of the highest rates in the world.

LIVING
STANDARD: GDP = US$2,200 per capita. Although living standards can be considered low, many Peruvian workers purchase homes, some with government assistance.

AGRICULTURE: Sugarcane, potatoes, rice, corn, wheat, beans, cassava, plantains, cotton, coffee, cocoa, wool, barley, sheep, cattle, pork, chickens and roundwood.

INDUSTRY:	Cement, flour, animal feed, sugar, sulfuric acid, cooking oil, urea, vehicles, mining, petroleum products, fishing, textiles, foodstuffs, light manufacturing and shipbuilding.

NATURAL
RESOURCES: Peru is rich in natural resources, including copper, silver, gold, petroleum, natural gas, timber, fish, iron ore, coal, phosphates, potash, zinc and lead. A major natural gas site is located in Camisea. Peru's high, clear, *altiplano* region is excellent for space observation and launching sites.

CLIMATE: Diverse, varying from very dry mountain areas to tropical rain forests. Peru lies entirely within the tropics. However, the Peru Current, an unusually cold ocean current, keeps the coast cooler than is normal for a tropical region. Lima's temperature is mild year round.

CURRENCY: Nuevo sol. 1 sol = 100 centimos.

THE PEOPLE

CORRECT
NAME: Peruvians.
Adjective: Peruvian.

ETHNIC
MAKEUP: 47 percent Quechua, 32 percent mestizo, 15 percent European (generally Spaniard), 5 percent Aymara, 1 percent other.

VALUE SYSTEM:	Peruvians are very proud of their country. Their strong will and desire to succeed have helped them overcome political and economic setbacks. Peruvians are very accommodating and have a good sense of humor.
FAMILY:	The family is very tight knit and supportive and is the cornerstone of every relationship at all levels of society.
RELIGION:	92 percent Roman Catholic, 8 percent other. Religion is very important in Peruvian life, and freedom of religion is guaranteed. Until 1979, Catholicism was the state religion, and the Catholic Church still plays a major role in people's lives. Many indigenous people combine Catholic beliefs with native religious beliefs. Many Protestant and evangelical churches operate in Peru.
EDUCATION:	School is compulsory from age seven to sixteen. The literacy rate is 87 percent among adults and higher among children. There are 35 universities throughout Peru. The University of San Marcos, established in Lima in 1551, is one of the oldest universities in the Western Hemisphere.
SPORTS:	Soccer is the most popular sport. Basketball, volleyball, tennis, golf and surfing are also widely enjoyed. *Frontón* is similar to racquetball and is played by men and women all over the country.

RECREATION: Family recreation includes picnics and movies. Sunday is a big day for outings and spending time together as a family. Music and dancing are very popular. Traditional Indian music attracts large crowds in cafes and dance halls. Hit tunes from the United States are also a favorite music. Movies are popular. Most major cities in Peru hold an annual festival (*feria*) to honor their patron saint. The festivals include religious processions, feasting, games and dancing.

IMPORTANT DATES

13th Century	The Incas begin to form their empire, centered at Cusco. Peru becomes the core of Incan culture.
1532	Spain invades Peru under Francisco Pizarro.
1533	Pizarro kills the last Incan ruler and enslaves the natives. Abundant mineral resources help the Peruvian region become the richest, most powerful Spanish colony in South America.
1535	Pizarro founds Lima.
1821-26	José de San Martín, with help from Simón Bolívar and Antonio de Sucre, leads Peru to victory and independence from Spain.
1879-84	Peru loses territory to Chile (War of the Pacific).
1929	Chile returns the Tacna region to Peru.
1933	A new constitution establishes a democratic government, but military and dictator rule become the norm.
1963	Fernando Belaúnde Terry is elected president in a free, multi-party election.
1968	Belaúnde is deposed by a military junta that controls Peru until 1980.

1968-1974	Military government institutes sweeping reforms in agriculture and nationalizes petroleum companies, mining companies and banks.
1980	A civilian government, elected by the people, begin working to increase private enterprise. The Shining Path begins its mission to overthrow the government by using violent terrorist tactics.
1985	Mismanagement worsens economic conditions.
1990	Alberto Fujimori is elected president.
1992	February: Fujimori dissolves Congress and suspends the constitution in an attempt to stabilize the economy.
	September: Shining Path leader Abimael Guzmán Reynoso is captured by the government. He and ten other guerrilla leaders are sentenced to life in prison.
	November: A new Constituent Assembly is elected to write a new constitution.
1995	Fujimori is re-elected president.
1996	In December, members of the Tupac Amaru movement—a leftist organization modeled after Fidel Castro's revolutionaries—pose as waiters to enter a reception at the Japanese ambassador's house. They take more than 500 attendees hostage, demanding the release of jailed comrades. Most of the hostages are released in the following months.
1997	April: Hostages rescued in army blitz. One hostage (of the 72 remaining) and all fourteen rebels die.

- More than eight million indigenous people live in Peru, more than any other country in the Western Hemisphere.

- Some of the largest trout in the world come from Lake Titicaca, the highest navigable water mass on earth.

- Legend has it that the red- and white-banded Peruvian flag was inspired when freedom fighter José de San Martín saw flamingos with white bodies and red wings take flight. He supposedly said, "Those shall be the colors of liberty."

- A sculpture of *Madre Patria* (Mother Country) in Lima is crowned with laurels— a common enough artistic device, except for the small head of an Andean llama peeking through the leaves. The sculptor had ordered his assistant to top the sculpture with a torchlight, which is *"llama"* in Spanish. The assistant got confused and used the animal head instead.

More than eight million indigenous people live in Peru.

See pages 63-67.

- Take the time necessary to offer a warm, friendly greeting.

- Shake hands when meeting and departing.

- Women greet female and male friends with one kiss on the right cheek. Business associates kiss only if they are also friends.

- Male friends may hug each other.

NAMES AND TITLES

See pages 69-75.

- Older people and businesspeople take titles very seriously. Younger people are more casual with the use of names and may not use titles.

- Friends address each other by their first names.

- Address people by their professional title: Doctor, Professor, Engineer, etc.

LANGUAGE

- Spanish and Quechua are the official languages.

- Two million Indians living in the highest parts of the Andes speak only Quechua, which is by far the most common Indian language. Thirty percent of Peruvians speak Quechua, Aymara or another native language but no Spanish.

- Most business people understand English. The well-educated and wealthy generally speak English.

- It is very important to maintain good eye contact while talking or listening.

- People stand close to one other. It is offensive to back away.

- It is common to walk arm in arm with good friends and family members.

- Men cross their legs at the knee, not the ankle. Only women cross their legs at the ankle, which is viewed as feminine.

GESTURES

- Some people point by pursing their lips and motioning in the desired direction.

- To beckon someone, extend your arm, palm down, and move your fingers back and forth.

- Tapping your head indicates "I'm thinking."

- Holding your hand flat and flicking toward someone or something means "go away."

- Tapping the index finger to the temple indicates "crazy."

BODY LANGUAGE

Men cross their legs at the knee, not the ankle.

Wagging your finger means "no."

LOCO LOCO

When my brother John visited Peru recently, a beautiful little girl befriended him and found him whenever he left his hotel. One day when he only had large bills in his pocket, this little girl approached him with her hand out and cried "change, change." John thought he knew exactly how to put an end to this situation without hurting her feelings. He proudly replied, "No peso poco, peso grande." He thought he was relaying that he didn't have any small change, so he was a little stunned when the cherub twirled her finger near the side of her head in the universal sign for crazy. "Loco, Señor," she giggled. Talking to his tour guide later, John found out he had told the little girl in his fractured Spanish, "I don't weigh a little, I weigh big!"

SMALL TALK

- Talk about the beauty and history of Peru, family, culture and politics.

- Do not give your opinion on local politics unless asked.

- Do not talk about racial prejudices or terrorists.

Never joke about the drug problem.

- Never ask anyone's ancestry or say "You look like an Inca."

- Never joke about the drug problem.

DINING AND SOCIAL EVENTS

- The main meal is served at midday.

- Dinner is generally served after 9:00 p.m. In Lima, the meal may not begin until after 10:00 p.m., but in smaller cities it is usually eaten earlier, around 7:00 p.m.

- Correct table manners are important. Politeness requires eating everything on your plate.

- Lively, casual conversation accompanies meals.

- Summon a waiter by waving.

Correct table manners are important.

FOOD

- Potatoes, peanuts, tomatoes and squash were first cultivated in Peru.

- Rice, fish, beans and fruit are the main dietary staples.

- Many Peruvian dishes are highly seasoned with onions and hot peppers.

TYPICAL FOODS

- *Pisco sour:* a lime - flavored alcoholic beverage, similar to a margarita. It originated in Peru and is the national drink.

- *Ceviche:* raw fish with lemon and vinegar, popular on the coast. It is the national dish of Peru.

- *Papa a la Huancaina:* a baked potato topped with eggs and a hot chili sauce.

- *Turrón de Doña Pepa:* an almond brittle candy that is a traditional Peruvian dessert.

TIPPING

- In restaurants a small tip is given even if a service charge is included in the bill. If a charge is not included, tip 15 percent.

- Tip taxi drivers at your discretion; it is not expected.

- Tip porters US$1 per bag in better hotels.

Tip taxi drivers at your discretion.

- Peruvians dress formally and conservatively.

DRESS

BUSINESS

- Men: Well-tailored suits, except on Saturdays, when more casual attire is acceptable.

- Women: Suits and dresses.

EVENING/ENTERTAINMENT

- Men: Dark suits.

- Women: Elegant dresses. Cocktail dresses and evening gowns are appropriate for more formal occasions. Peruvian women have their hair, make-up and nails professionally done for a party.

Peruvian women have their hair, make-up and nails professionally done for a party.

CASUAL

- Men: Nice slacks and shirts.

- Women: Pants, skirts and blouses.

- Tennis shoes should only be worn when exercising.

- Fashionable jeans may be appropriate for certain occasions.

Fashionable jeans may be appropriate for certain occasions.

GIFTS

- Be aware of the "caste" system in Peru. Family history, social position and education may influence the appropriateness of a gift.

- Flowers are an appropriate gift for any occasion.

- Do not give thirteen of anything, purple or black objects, knives or handkerchiefs.

HOSTESS

- Give gifts from your state or country, wine, liquors, chocolates and flowers, especially roses.

- Do not give red roses unless romance is intended.

- A gift for the children is appreciated. T-shirts, caps and cassette tapes make good gifts.

BUSINESS

- Gifts are an important part of business protocol but are not required at the first meeting.

- Present a gift at a social occasion, not a business meeting.

- Give imported alcohol (it is expensive), calculators, electronic address books, date books or daytimers, name brand pen sets, ties and scarves.

- Your company logo should be understated if used on a gift.

- Peru is more conservative and less modern than Brazil, Argentina and Chile.

DO

- Peruvians take great pride in both Indian and Spanish heritage. Learn some history and ask your colleagues informed questions.

If you smoke or chew gum, offer cigarettes or candy to your counterparts first.

- If you smoke or chew gum, offer cigarettes or candy to your counterparts first. Sharing is very important.

DO NOT

- Do not bring up terrorism, the Shining Path or the Tupac Amaru. If your counterparts discuss these topics, listen and ask questions, but refrain from giving your opinion.

- Do not discuss poverty. Peruvians are very proud of what they have accomplished and feel they have come a long way in this area.

- Do not wear native dress.

- Do not take photographs of Indians without asking permission. People in the villages and mountains believe that photographing children steals their souls.

Never change money with street-side moneychangers.

- Never change money with street-side moneychangers. Counterfeit bills in U.S. currency are common. Change money only at a bank. You will need your passport.

PUNCTUALITY AND PACE

- The concept of time is relaxed, and people are more important than schedules.

- Be on time for business meetings, doctor appointments and airline flights, but be prepared to wait.

- It is polite to be at least thirty minutes late for dinner and later for social occasions. People will be surprised and not pleased if you arrive on time.

- Only a bullfight requires punctuality.

STRICTLY BUSINESS

CORPORATE CULTURE

- The *"cargo"* is a series of ranked offices with specific duties. Participation in this system is essential to one's wealth and status.

"What is your *cargo?*" means "What is your position?"

- North Americans will be welcomed and well received. Foreign investment is vital to Peru's future.

MEETINGS

- Meetings may not start on time.

- Be sure to include several materials (graphics, computers, etc.) and use a variety of visual aids in your presentations.

COMMUNICATION

- Print all business materials in Spanish and English. Present business plans in Spanish, if possible.

- Your Peruvian counterparts will much prefer dealing with you in person rather than by fax or phone. Plan on taking several trips to conclude a deal.

- Peruvians negotiate with individuals, not an organization. Always allow the same negotiators to continue until the process ends. Changing representatives will halt or end the process.

Rule of Thumb

Your Peruvian counterparts will much prefer dealing with you in person.

- Be flexible and patient. Data may be reviewed several times. Never be confrontational.

Establish a relationship with a local mediator.

- It is acceptable to use e-mail for business communication. Do not expect a quick response to your e-mail, however.

BE AWARE

- Establish a relationship with a local mediator. This person will be invaluable in helping you through the complicated networks of business and government.

- The average workweek in Peru—48 hours—is one of the longest in the world.

Faux Pas

Business is not discussed over dinner.

ENTERTAINMENT

- Appearances are important; choose prestigious restaurants for entertaining.

- Spouses are invited to business dinners.

- Business is not discussed over dinner. Do not bring it up unless your host initiates the conversation.

- Business entertaining and hosting almost always lead to drinking. Do not order imported alcohol if you are the guest. It is very expensive.

- Dinner invitations are seldom before 9:00 p.m., with dinner served at 10:30 p.m.

- Arrive thirty minutes late, and stay at least thirty minutes after dinner.

APPOINTMENTS

- Make appointments two weeks in advance.

- Do not stop by unannounced at business or government offices.

- Try to schedule appointments in the morning. Meetings may extend into lunch, so don't schedule more than one in a single morning.

Do not stop by unannounced at business or government offices.

BUSINESS HOURS

- Businesses and offices are generally open from 8:00 a.m. to 5:00 or 6:00 p.m.

- Some small businesses close from 1:00 to 3:00 p.m. for siesta.

- Banks are open Monday through Friday from 9:00 a.m. to 6:00 p.m. Many banks are also open Saturdays until 1:00 p.m.

Winter hours may be half an hour to an hour longer.

- Do not schedule meetings in the summer vacation period from January to March or during the two weeks before and after Christmas and Easter.

ESPECIALLY FOR WOMEN

While Peruvian women have traditionally been subservient to men, this is changing. Today's educated women are much more aggressive. An increasing number of women are running companies and working in government and business.

Ignore all advances and comments from strangers.

- Men are used to doing business with other men. It may take time for a woman to be accepted by men in the business community.

- Unescorted women may be viewed negatively. It is best to travel in groups.

HEALTH AND SAFETY

- Quality health care is given in expensive private clinics.

- Drink bottled water.

- Be aware of malaria and other tropical diseases in the jungle areas. Consider getting vaccinations before leaving the United States.

Take precautions against the effects of the high altitude.

- Take precautions against the effects of the high altitude.

- Register with your embassy upon arrival.

- Upon arrival, contact the Lima Tourist Police (71-45-769) or the South American

Explorers Club (31-44-80) for the latest information on unsafe areas.

- Always carry your passport. Report its loss immediately to the local police and the U.S. Embassy.

- Pickpockets and armed robbery are common problems. Thieves will try to divert your attention; don't be distracted by your surroundings.

Be very careful at a cash machine or bank.

- Tourists are especially vulnerable. Try not to look like a tourist or North American.

- Never carry large amounts of cash, wear flashy jewelry or display valuables. Use a money belt, and try not to carry anything in your hands.

- Be very careful at a cash machine or bank. Be sure no one is watching you.

Call ahead to order a cab from a home or your hotel.

- Call ahead to order a cab from a home or your hotel. Do not hail a cab in the street.

- Don't travel off the beaten track or alone. Don't go where the Peruvian government or your hosts advise you not to go.

HOLIDAYS AND FESTIVALS

Do not plan to make a business visit or schedule any appointments during the following holidays or festivals. Be sure to check for the numerous regional and local holidays and festivals.

January	New Year's Day (1)
March/April	Holy Thursday (varies)
	Good Friday (varies)
	Easter (varies)
May	Labor Day (1)
June	The Day of Race (24)
	Saints Peter and Paul (29)
July	Independence Day (28)
	National Day (29)
August	St. Rose of Lima (30)
October	Navy Day; Battle of Angamos (8)
November	All Saints' Day (1)
December	Feast of the Immaculate Conception (8)
	Christmas Day (25)

Visit the October fair in Lima. Festivities last the entire month of October.

• Local holidays honor special saints, celebrate agricultural seasons or provide general recreation.

• The Day of Race celebrates the pride of Inca history. It is an especially big event in Cusco and is celebrated with music, dancing, food and festivities.

27.

URUGUAY
ORIENTAL REPUBLIC OF URUGUAY

VITAL STATISTICS

POPULATION: 3,223,000. The growth rate is 0.74 percent, the lowest in South America.

CAPITAL: Montevideo, with a population of 1.5 million. Almost half the population of Uruguay lives in Montevideo.

MAJOR CITIES: Salto (81,000), Paysandú (75,000).

GEOGRAPHY: 72,172 square miles (176,220 square kilometers), slightly smaller than Oklahoma.

GOVERNMENT: Republic, composed of 19 departments. The president is the chief of state and head of government and cannot be elected for two consecutive terms. The bicameral General

Assembly is composed of a 99-member Chamber of Deputies and a 30-member Senate. Voting is compulsory for all citizens eighteen years of age and older. People must return to their place of birth to vote.

ECONOMY: Uruguay was historically one of the most stable and wealthiest nations in South America. The majority of the people are middle class; the extremes of wealth and poverty found in most other South American countries don't exist. Uruguay has the best-educated workforce on the continent.

Economic conditions declined in the 1970s and 1980s under military rule. The 1990s have seen Uruguay's economy improve under programs to cut the budget deficit and privatize some state-owned businesses. The economy remains dependent on agriculture, which comprises more than 50 percent of Uruguayan exports. Uruguay is a member of Mercosur.

LIVING
STANDARD: GDP = US$6,070 per capita.

AGRICULTURE: Wheat, rice, corn, sugarcane, sugar beets, fruits, vegetables, sorghum, sheep, cattle, horses and roundwood. Uruguay's greatest natural resource is its fertile land. More than 80 percent of the land is used in agriculture and livestock production. Uruguay is a world leader in cattle and wool production.

INDUSTRY:	Foodstuffs, beverages, petroleum products, chemicals, vehicles, tobacco products, paper products, wool, hides and skins, cement, meat processing, leather production, textiles, leather footwear, handbags, leather apparel and fish processing.
NATURAL RESOURCES:	Arable land, hydroelectric power, gypsum and fishing. Uruguay has few mineral resources. Gravel, sand and stone are the leading mineral products.
CLIMATE:	Mild and humid, with little variation from region to region.
CURRENCY:	Peso Uruguayo. 1 peso = 100 centesimos.

THE PEOPLE

Correct Name:	Uruguayans. Adjective: Uruguayan.
ETHNIC MAKEUP:	88 percent European (Spanish and Italian), 8 percent mestizo, 4 percent black. There are almost no indigenous people in Uruguay.
VALUE SYSTEM:	Uruguayans take a pragmatic, utilitarian and materialistic approach to life. They have an inherent trust in people and a strong belief in

social justice. Self-identity is based on a person's role in the social system and the history of his or her extended family. Individuals are responsible for their decisions, and individualism is respected. People are equal because each person is deemed unique. The small upper class controls much of the wealth and commerce, but the large middle class is very influential. A person can be socially upper class and not have much money.

FAMILY: Strong ties unite the family. The father plays an important role as patriarch, but a great deal of the family responsibility is given to the mother. Unless they attend a college or university, children usually stay at home until they marry.

RELIGION: 66 percent Roman Catholic, 2 percent Protestant, 2 percent Jewish, 30 percent non-professing or other. Uruguay is the most secular of South American countries. Less than half the adult population attends church regularly, although Catholicism is an integral part of the national culture. Church and state are strictly separated and religious freedom is guaranteed by the constitution.

EDUCATION: A great deal of emphasis is placed on education. People enjoy easy access to a good education, compulsory for nine years and free through post-graduate studies. The literacy rate is 96 percent, one of the highest in South America.

SPORTS: *Fútbol* (soccer) is the national sport. The first World Cup was held in Uruguay in 1930—and won by Uruguay. In the 1950 World Cup,

Uruguay upset a favored Brazil in Rio de Janeiro. It is said that Uruguayans who weren't even born at the time can recall this exciting game. Basketball, volleyball, swimming, rowing and other water sports are also popular. Middle and upper class families play paddle, a game similar to tennis. *Fútbol 5* is indoor soccer.

RECREATION: Music is popular. Older people like tango, folk music and jazz, while the younger set favors rock. Cultural events, movies and family barbecues are favorite pastimes. Uruguayans spend a great deal of time at the magnificent beaches along the Atlantic coast.

IMPORTANT DATES

Pre-16th Century	Charúas, a native tribe, inhabit the land.
1516	Spanish explorers first visit the area.
1624	The first settlement is established at Soriano.
1680-1726	Portuguese are present in the area.
1726	The Spanish begin to colonize Uruguay. They drive out the Portuguese and kill or drive out almost all of the indigenous people.
1811	War of Independence. José Gervasio Artigas, the Father of Uruguay, leads his country against the Spanish for five years. The drive for independence is unsuccessful.
1821	The Spanish rule effectively ends when Portugal annexes Uruguay to Brazil.
1825	The "Thirty-three Immortals" revolt and declare Uruguay an independent republic.

1828	Uruguay gains freedom from Brazil; independence is granted.
1839-1851	Civil War.
1865-1870	War with Paraguay.
1903	José Batlle y Ordóñez becomes the first freely elected president. He changes the constitution to allow himself to serve until 1929.
1905	Women are given the right to vote. Divorce is legalized.
1970	Severe economic conditions lead to terrorist violence and unrest.
1973	Military coup ousts President Juan M. Bordaberry. Thirteen years of military rule follow, during which thousands are detained and tortured, and 10 percent of the population flee into exile.
1980	Elections are held and the vote goes against the military, which nullifies the vote and appoints General Gregorio Alvarez president.
1984	The military relinquishes control.
1985	Colorado party leader Julio Maria Sanguinetti is elected to office. The government grants amnesty to persons suspected of human rights violations in order to avoid clashes with the military. Basic human rights are restored.
1989	Luis Alberto Lacalle Herrera is elected in the first democratic transfer of power from one elected government to another since 1971.
1994	Julio Maria Sanguinetti returns to office for another five-year term.
1999	Presidential elections scheduled.

- Uruguay was the first South American country to give women the right to vote (1905) and among the first to legalize divorce.

- You will see many "classic" cars in Uruguay, since purchasing and insuring a new vehicle is prohibitively expensive. A new, modest car costs the average worker the equivalent of eight years' salary. You will see De Sotos, Studebakers, and even Ford Model As in running order. The streets are a museum of old cars.

MEETING AND GREETING

See pages 63-67.

- Greetings are warm and accompanied by a firm handshake.

- Friends kiss once on the right cheek when meeting.

- Generally men will not kiss women in a business setting.

- Friends and family embrace when meeting.

- People do not greet strangers when passing on the street. Greeting or smiling at a stranger may be misunderstood.

Friends kiss once on the right cheek when meeting.

NAMES AND TITLES

See pages 69-75.

- Only children, family members and close friends address each other by their first names.

- Everyone who graduates from a university, at any level, is entitled to be addressed as "Doctor."

- People generally do not use Don or Doña, except in diplomatic circles.

LANGUAGE

- Spanish is the official language. A little Italian is mixed in with Uruguayan Spanish.

Uruguayans have a very distinct accent.

- Uruguayans have a very distinct accent; it is quite different from that heard in other Spanish speaking countries. For example, Uruguayans pronounce *y* and *ll* as "sh."

- A general knowledge of English is found in commercial and government circles.

- *Brazilero*—a Portuguese-Spanish mix—is spoken on the Brazilian frontier.

- Uruguayans stand very close when conversing, both socially and in business.

- People touch shoulders and hold arms while they talk to each other.

- Never sit on or put your feet up on a ledge, desk or table.

- Try not to yawn, especially in business settings. Yawning indicates that one is disinterested or sleepy.

- A man should offer his seat to a woman on public transportation.

*The
North American
"O.K." sign is
extremely rude.*

GESTURES

- The "ch-ch" sound is used to get someone's attention or to get a bus to stop.

- The North American "O.K." sign is extremely rude.

- The "thumbs up" gesture means "O.K."

- You may see people brush the backs of their hands under their chins to signal "I don't know."

SMALL TALK

- Uruguayans love to talk and everyone speaks at the same time.

- Talk about cultural traditions, history and sports—especially soccer.

- Uruguayans are extremely political people. Ask about politics.

- Ask questions about Uruguay. People are very proud of their country.

- Don't confuse Paraguay and Uruguay!

PHRASES

See page 80.

DINING AND SOCIAL EVENTS

- Uruguayans usually dine at 9:00 or 10:00 p.m.

- Keep your hands above the table and elbows off the table.

- Taking a second helping shows appreciation for the food.

- When finished eating, place your utensils side by side on your plate. Dinner guests remain at the table until everyone is finished eating.

- It is extremely impolite to use a toothpick in public.

- Raise your hand to signal for a waiter. Some locals may use a kissing sound to summon a waiter, but this is considered rude.

- If a Uruguayan invites you to his or her home for coffee after dinner, don't stay late on a work night. Be alert for cues from your counterparts telling you they are tired and want to end the night.

Faux Pas

It is extremely impolite to use a toothpick in public.

FOOD

- Uruguay produces most of its own food.

- Some of the best beef in the world is raised in Uruguay.

- Varieties of fish, meat, vegetables and fruit are available.

- Wheat and rice are the primary grains.

- Pizza and pasta are excellent in Uruguay.

Some of the best beef in the world is raised in Uruguay.

- Uruguayans eat more than 200 pounds of meat per capita each year. Beef is consumed almost every day. Roasts, stews and meat pies are popular menu items.

TYPICAL FOODS

- *Guiso:* ground beef with rice, onion and egg.

- *Milanesas:* breaded, fried steak.

- *Asado:* grilled beef.

- *Chivito:* steak and eggs with cheese and mayonnaise.

- *Parrillada criolla:* a mixture of barbecued sausages, kidneys and strips of beef.

- *Maté:* a tea brewed from the dried leaves of a native holly tree. It is the national beverage.

TIPPING

- In a restaurant, tip 10 percent if no service charge is included in the bill.

- Tip taxis 10 percent.

- Tip porters US $1.

US dollars are widely accepted.

DRESS

- Uruguayans dress conservatively, seldom wearing the bright colors popular elsewhere in South America.

- Bring appropriate clothing for the warm, humid summer and rainy, chilly winter.

- Women may not wear nylons during the summer.

- If your Uruguayan colleagues do not wear ties or jackets in the summer, you may follow.

- Drenching pedestrians with water is a favorite prank of the young during Carnival; dress accordingly.

Drenching pedestrians with water is a favorite prank of the young during Carnival.

BUSINESS

- Men: Conservative, dark suits and ties.

- Women: Blouses with dark suits, skirts and dresses.

EVENING/ENTERTAINMENT

- Men: Dark suits. Many restaurants require a coat and tie.

- Women: Dresses and skirts. Cocktail dresses are appropriate for the theater and formal dinner parties.

CASUAL

- Men: Jackets and blazers.

- Women: Skirts, pants, designer jeans.

- Both men and women wear pants in casual situations.

- Clean, fashionable jeans are acceptable casual wear.

- Women should not wear shorts except at the beach.

GIFTS

- Everyone likes North American jeans.

- Women love flowers, especially roses. A rare salmon-colored tea rose is a favorite.

HOSTESS

Gift giving is not an important part of doing business.

- It is common for guests to send candy or flowers to a hostess before the occasion.

BUSINESS

- Gift giving is not an important part of doing business.

- Give scotch (Black Label or Chivas Regal) and gifts made in the United States, especially from your region.

DO

- A Tourist Card will be issued to you when you enter the country (usually on the plane), and you must keep it until you leave.

- Make sure to make time to visit a ranch. Uruguayan ranches are beautiful and a visit makes a wonderful holiday for adults and children.

DO NOT

- Do not visit Montevideo during the International Cattle Show and Industrial Exhibition in August. It is very difficult to get a hotel room.

- A highly trained and educated businessperson may be working at a low-level position due to exile, imprisonment or political affiliation. Do not ask questions.

- Do not change money at casinos. The exchange rate is terrible.

- Punctuality is not a high priority.

- Be on time for business meetings.

HELPFUL HINTS

Make sure to make time to visit a ranch.

PUNCTUALITY AND PACE

- People are very casual about time for social events. An invitation for 9:00 p.m. usually means to arrive by 10:00 p.m.

- When people invite you to their home they may say "Come at 8:00, 8:30, 9:00."

STRICTLY BUSINESS

CORPORATE CULTURE

- The small upper class intermarries within itself and continues to control most of the wealth and commerce.

Kinship and friendship play a major role in business.

- Kinship and friendship play a major role in business transactions. Expertise and experience are less important than who you are.

- Personal loyalty is more important than any company or institution.

- Uruguayan executives will be experienced and sophisticated; they may have studied in the United States or Europe.

Meetings are extremely formal but don't usually start on time.

MEETINGS

- Meetings are extremely formal but don't usually start on time.

- Present business cards to everyone in a meeting.

- Be ready to make small talk before the business discussions begin.

COMMUNICATION

- Many executives will speak English, but arrange for an interpreter.

- Print all materials in Spanish, from business cards to brochures.

- E-mail is an acceptable form of business communication, but do not expect e-mail to be responded to promptly.

BE AWARE

- Hire a local contact to help you in the business community and to navigate you through red tape.

ENTERTAINMENT

- Take your business colleagues to an international hotel or a high quality French, Chinese or Uruguayan restaurant for dinner.

- Business lunches are common. Uruguayans are comfortable conducting business over lunch.

Hire a local contact to help you in the business community.

Business lunches are common.

- Business dinners are to socialize. Do not talk business unless your host initiates the conversation.

- An invitation to a casino is not unusual.

APPOINTMENTS

- Most business people in Uruguay put in a very long business day.

- You won't get any business done during elections. Before the elections, people go to meetings, and all offices and businesses are closed on election day.

- The best time of year to conduct business is from May through November. Little business is conducted in the two weeks before and after Christmas and Easter, or during Carnival.

BUSINESS HOURS

- Businesses are open Monday through Friday from 8:30 a.m. to noon and from 2:30 p.m. to 6:30 p.m.

- Government offices are open Monday through Friday from 8:00 a.m. to 1:30 p.m. from November to mid-March and from noon to 6:30 p.m. the rest of the year.

- Bank hours are 1:00 p.m. to 5:00 p.m.

You won't get any business done during elections.

Little business is conducted during Carnival.

Women are considered equal to men in all respects. They have equal job and educational opportunities. Uruguayan women are well-educated, and there are many women in the professions and high government offices. The Minister of Labor is a woman. Almost all women work outside the home.

Men like to be with and enjoy doing business with women.

- A foreign woman will have no problem doing business in Uruguay. It may even be an advantage. Men like to be with and enjoy doing business with women.

- Do not misinterpret an invitation to join a man for a business lunch. He is not attempting to seduce you.

- Do not be shocked if you meet a man for business and he shakes your hand and kisses your cheek. This is a normal greeting.

- Uruguay has good health standards, and modern facilities are available in Montevideo.

- The streets of Montevideo are safe.

- Be careful of pickpockets on buses.

The streets of Montevideo are safe.

HOLIDAYS AND FESTIVALS

Do not plan to make a business visit or schedule any appointments during the following holidays or festivals. Be sure to check for the numerous regional and local holidays and festivals.

January	New Year's Day (1)
	Epiphany (6)
February/March	Carnival (the Monday and Tuesday before Ash Wednesday, varies)
March/April	Holy Week (varies)
	Easter (varies)
April	Landing of the Thirty-three Patriots (19)
May	Labor Day (1)
	Battle of Las Piedras (18)
June	Birthday of José Gervasio Artigas (19)
July	Constitution Day (18)
August	Independence Day (25)
October	Columbus Day (12)
November	All Saints' Day (1)
December	Feast of the Immaculate Conception (8)
	Christmas (25)

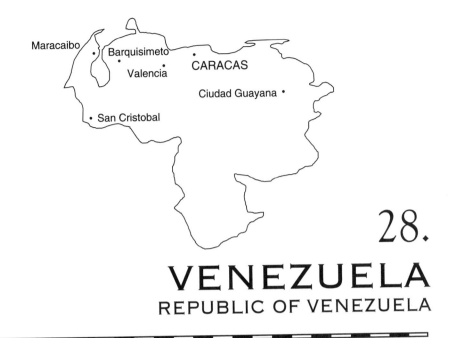

28.

VENEZUELA
REPUBLIC OF VENEZUELA

VITAL STATISTICS

POPULATION: 21,005,000. Venezuela is one of the least densely populated nations in the Western Hemisphere with only nine people per square kilometer.

CAPITAL: Caracas, with a population of 3.3 million.

MAJOR CITIES: Maracaibo (1,151,933), Valencia (889,228), Barquisimeto (681,961).

GEOGRAPHY: 352,143 square miles (912,050 square kilometers), roughly twice the size of California. Venezuela is composed of four geographical areas: the Caribbean coastal area, where 90 percent of the population lives; the Andes Mountains in the west; the Central Plains; and the Guyana Highlands.

GOVERNMENT:	Federal Republic, composed of 21 states, one territory, one federal district and one federal dependency. The president is the head of government and chief of state. The bicameral Congress of the Republic is composed of a 53-seat Senate and 203-seat Chamber of Deputies. All citizens eighteen and older may vote.
ECONOMY:	Venezuela is working to privatize state industries, attract foreign investment and liberalize trade. Economic controls that discourage foreign and domestic investment are under review. Venezuela is a founding member of OPEC. Despite efforts to diversify, petroleum is the biggest influence on and contribution to the economy. Oil accounts for 70 percent of all export earnings.
	Venezuela has a higher standard of living than many South American countries due to its petroleum production. Dependence on petroleum, however, has caused some economic instability.
LIVING STANDARD:	GDP = US$4,490 per capita.
AGRICULTURE:	Rice, coffee, corn, sugar, bananas, dairy, meats and poultry products.
INDUSTRY:	Oil refining, petrochemicals, iron and steel, paper products, aluminum, textiles, transport equipment and consumer products. Orimulsion, an environmentally important petroleum product used in power plants, is produced only in Venezuela.

NATURAL
RESOURCES: Petroleum is the most important natural resource. Others include natural gas, coal, iron ore, gold, other minerals, hydroelectric power and bauxite.

CLIMATE: Venezuela lies entirely within the tropics, but average temperatures vary throughout the country due to changes in elevation.

CURRENCY: Bolívar. 1 bolívar = 100 centimos.

THE PEOPLE

CORRECT
NAME: Venezuelans.
Adjective: Venezuelan.

ETHNIC
MAKEUP: 67 percent mestizo, 21 percent European, 10 percent black, 2 percent Amerindian.

Venezuela has been a magnet for immigrants. Large numbers of Europeans settled in Venezuela during World War II. In the 1970s there was an influx of immigrants from other Latin American and Caribbean countries. Venezuelans are very proud of their ethnic mixture and all races are considered equal. There are fewer than 20,000 indigenous Venezuelans.

VALUE SYSTEM:	Venezuelans respect leadership and are tolerant and loving. Family, extended family and friends are very important, and one must not do anything to shame them. The farther you go from the cities, the friendlier the people become. The upper class dominates the economic structures of commerce and industry, but the middle class dominates politics.
FAMILY:	The extended family gives people a sense of security. Family ties are strong, and most families are close-knit, especially among the upper and middle classes. The father dominates in Venezuelan homes, and the mother is responsible for raising the children and managing the household.
RELIGION:	95 percent Roman Catholic, 3 percent Protestant, 2 percent other. People are emotionally attached to the church, which gives them a sense of stability, but religion is not a strong force in daily life. Venezuelans are very proud of the fact that religious freedom is guaranteed by the constitution.
EDUCATION:	Education is compulsory for nine years. All education, including university level, is free in government-financed institutions. Twenty percent of the national budget is spent on education, one of the highest rates in the world. The literacy rate is 90 percent.

SPORTS:	The most popular spectator sport is baseball. Professional basketball and soccer are also favorites. People attend horse races and bullfights.
RECREATION:	Venezuela is one of the most popular and best fishing areas in the world, especially in the Guri Lakes region. Venezuelans like to dance, especially the merengue and salsa, and go to the beach, movies and cultural events. Rock music is popular among young people. Playing dominos and bolas, similar to bocce ball, is widespread.

IMPORTANT DATES

Pre-16th Century	Native Americans, including the Caracas, Arawaks and Cumanagatos, inhabit the area.
1498	Columbus lands at Paria on his third voyage, the first European to visit South America.
1516	Nueva Cadiz, on the Island of Cubagua, is founded, becoming the first European city in South America.
1811	Venezuela declares independence, beginning a ten year conflict with Spain. One-quarter of the population dies in wars over the next fourteen years.
1821	Simón Bolívar leads his forces to victory over Spain at the Battle of Carabobo. Venezuela joins the federation of Gran Colombia.

1830	Venezuela forms a separate, independent republic.
1859-1863	Federal War, the most devastating of a series of internal struggles.
1908-1935	The repressive dictatorship of Juan Vicente Gómez unifies Venezuela under a central government.
1947	Rómulo Gallegos becomes the first popularly elected president but is overthrown by a military coup nine months later.
1958	Civilian rule returns after ten years of military rule.
1976	Venezuela nationalizes the petroleum industry and compensates companies.
1989	Carlos Andrés Pérez becomes president. Government-mandated price increases spark riots in which 300 people are killed.
1992	Two attempted coups fail to overthrow the government.
1993	Pérez is impeached for misusing government security funds. Rafael Caldera is elected president.
1998	Presidential elections are scheduled.

- The native stilt houses on the coast reminded an early explorer of Venice, which led to the name *Venezuela* or "Little Venice."

- Venezuela was the first South American colony to revolt against Spain.

- Venezuela produces one of the most sought-after flavors of chocolate in the world, called *chuao*. Several Swiss candy companies, as well as Godiva, buy this special chocolate.

- The world's highest waterfall is Angel Falls. It takes seventeen seconds for a drop of water to fall the length of the falls.

- Four Miss Universes and four Miss Worlds have come from Venezuela.

Venezuela produces one of the most sought-after flavors of chocolate in the world, called chuao.

See pages 63-67.

- Greetings are warm and friendly.

- Men greet friends with an embrace and a pat on the back. Women greet friends with an embrace and a kiss on the cheek.

- People kiss business acquaintances on the cheek once and personal friends twice.

- Handshakes are common among strangers.

NAMES AND TITLES	See pages 69-75 • People use the title "Doctor" for anyone who has graduated from a university. • Don and Doña are used for the elderly and members of the academy.
LANGUAGE	• Spanish is the official language and is spoken by almost everyone. • English is a required language in the schools. • It is not uncommon to hear Portuguese spoken, especially in Caracas. • Germans from the Black Forest speak their own language, similar to Dutch.

Germans from the Black Forest speak their own language.

BODY LANGUAGE	• Venezuelans stand very close when speaking. Do not back away. • Seating posture is important. Try to keep both feet on the floor and avoid slouching. Don't put your feet on furniture.
A TOUCHING SESSION	*Casual touching is common among males. The president of Venezuela, a big powerful man, didn't hesitate to step down from his seat in front of the Senate to kiss his son, a senator, during a recent emotional vote.*

GESTURES

- Pointing with your index finger can be considered rude. Motioning with your entire hand is more polite.

- Venezuelans will be familiar with North American gestures.

- People enjoy gathering in groups and talking.

- Always maintain eye contact when talking.

- Talk about business, art, literature and history. Ask questions about the Guri Dam, a point of national pride.

- Learn about Venezuelan history and politics and ask questions. Venezuelans love their country and will appreciate your interest.

- People call each other names like *Negro* ("black"), *Gordo* ("fatso"), *Chino* ("Chinaman"), etc. These nicknames are meant to show friendship, fondness and fun. They are not demeaning.

- Don't talk about local unrest, politics and inflation. Do not give your opinion on local politics.

SMALL TALK

Venezuelans love their country and will appreciate your interest.

PHRASES See page 80.

DINING AND SOCIAL EVENTS

Wait for everyone to be served before you start eating.

- Both the continental style and the United States' style of eating are used.

- Wait for everyone to be served before you start eating. You will normally be served a great deal of food and drink; people enjoy both but do not abuse either.

- When not using your utensils, rest the tips on the edge of the plate with the handles resting on the table. When you are finished eating, lay your knife and fork across your plate diagonally in the 5:25 position.

- The host sits at the head of the table and pays the check.

- The head and the foot of the table are usually reserved for the mother and father.

- Parties always include music, dancing, food and drinks.

- Birthdays are a *big* deal, even first and second birthdays. Caterers are hired, and music and dancing are always part of the event.

FOOD

- Much of the Venezuelan diet consists of hot foods, casseroles, meat pies, stews, pasta dishes, rice and corn-based dishes.

- Hot chocolate is very popular, almost as popular as coffee.

- In most cities there are open markets that provide a large variety of tropical fruits and fresh vegetables.

- A variety of excellent ethnic food is available, including Chinese, Italian, French and Spanish.

- Caracas has wonderful bakeries (*panadarías*). Try the baked goods.

- Venezuelans make very good coffee and there are at least thirty different varieties available. You can order the strength and flavor you enjoy.

- You may be served *un cafecito* (a thick black coffee) in a very small cup. Accept this graciously—it is a sign of hospitality and way of offering friendship.

There are at least thirty varieties of coffee available to try.

TYPICAL FOODS

- *Arepa:* a grilled, baked or deep-fried thick pancake made with white corn flour and filled with meat, cheese or whatever you like.

- *Punta trasera:* a tender steak that is a favorite.

- *Pabellón criollo:* made from black beans, rice, shredded meat and plantains (bananas).

- *Hallaca:* cornmeal dough filled with a variety of foods and cooked in wrappers made of banana leaves. It is the national dish, served mostly at Christmas.

TIPPING

- In restaurants, a 10 percent service charge is usually added to the bill, but an additional 5 percent tip is also expected. If a tip is not included in the bill, tip 10 percent.

- Don't tip taxi drivers.

- Tip porters US$1 per bag.

- A tip is sometimes required in advance to expedite a needed service.

A tip is sometimes required in advance to expedite a needed service.

- Venezuelans are very fashion conscious, and the latest European styles are worn in the cities.

- Appearances count. It is important to be neat, clean and properly groomed.

- Your watch and jewelry will be noticed.

- Cotton clothing is the most common and comfortable choice in the summer.

- Native people may wear European dress, traditional dress or a combination of both, depending on how much contact they maintain with the mestizo society. Do not dress like the natives.

Venezuelans are very fashion conscious.

BUSINESS

- Men: Conservative dark suits. Tropical weight wool is best for summer.

- Women: Feminine business suits, dresses, skirts and blouses.

EVENING/ENTERTAINMENT

- Men: Dark suits and ties.

- Women: An elegant cocktail dress will be required in more formal situations.

CASUAL

- Shorts and swimwear are only worn in recreation areas and at the beach.

- Clean, fashionable jeans are worn by men and women.

GIFTS

- Service personnel—garbage collectors, postal employees, etc.—may present a calling card requesting a gift of money at Christmas time. If you value the service, give the gift.

- White, gold and silver are popular colors for any gift.

HOSTESS

- Never visit anyone's home without bringing a gift.

- A gift for the children will be appreciated. A little dress or teddy bear would be appropriate.

- Send flowers before a social occasion. The orchid is the national flower.

- Give high-quality scotch or wine. Venezuelans love scotch.

White, gold and silver are popular colors for any gift.

BUSINESS

- Do not give gifts in business until a personal relationship has been established.

- Give good scotch (Johnny Walker Black Label, Chivas Regal), wine and unique electrical equipment.

- People are very North Americanized due to the oil companies (Mobil, Texaco, etc.), which have been in Venezuela for years.

DO

- A Plaza Bolívar, named after the greatly respected liberator, is found in all Venezuelan cities. Behave respectfully in any of these plazas.

- In airports, expect long lines and security checks by armed soldiers.

- Be sure to carry your passport at all times.

- Learn about Venezuelan baseball teams. Baseball is the most popular sport in Venezuela.

HELPFUL HINTS

Privacy is not valued in the same way it is in North America.

- Never use the term "mestizo" in Venezuela. People are not classified by racial mix or religion.

- Never eat while walking in the street.

PUNCTUALITY AND PACE

- Be punctual for business meetings, but be prepared to wait for your Venezuelan counterparts. The pace of business is relaxed, easygoing and informal. Be patient.

- Traffic can be a serious problem in Caracas. Allow sufficient time for travel.

Traffic can be a serious problem in Caracas.

- For social events, always arrive at least half an hour to an hour later than the invitation reads.

- VIPs arrive very late for social occasions in order to make an entrance.

STRICTLY BUSINESS

- Focus on long term relationships. Get to know your business colleagues personally before attempting to do business.

- Establish a local contact to make introductions. This contact should make introductions at the appropriate levels for business and social meetings.

CORPORATE CULTURE

- Family relationships are a dominant factor in business. Who your family is and whom you know is very important. Nepotism is a way of life.

- Clearly communicate your position and title in your company to communicate your status.

Family relationships are a dominant factor in business.

MEETINGS

- There will be minimal small talk before a meeting. Unlike other South Americans, Venezuelans will get right to the point.

- Venezuelans like to be in control. Don't push the process or dominate at business meetings.

- Negotiations will proceed slowly with many interruptions. Keep your sense of humor.

Keep your sense of humor.

COMMUNICATION

- Print all of your materials in Spanish.

- Presentations should be factual and realistic. You will deal with shrewd business people who will insist on being clear about a deal.

- It's better to do business in person than over the telephone.

- E-mail and computers are becoming more common but are not yet mainstream. Do not expect a quick response to your e-mail correspondence.

BE AWARE

- Never correct or embarrass anyone publicly.

ENTERTAINMENT

- Business entertaining is generally done in restaurants.

- Meals are for socializing. Don't discuss business unless your host initiates it.

APPOINTMENTS

- Make appointments two weeks in advance and reconfirm upon arrival.

- Avoid making business trips during January and February, when many people go on holiday.

BUSINESS HOURS

- Offices are generally open from 8:00 a.m. to 6:00 p.m., with a one or two hour midday break, Monday through Friday. These hours are rather flexible, due to heavy traffic conditions in larger cities.

- Government offices have hours similar to those of businesses, but vary regionally.

- In Caracas, banks are open Monday through Friday from 8:30 a.m. to 11:30 a.m. and 2:00 p.m. to 4:30 p.m. Banking hours vary in other cities.

Although machismo is strong, the status of women is higher in Venezuela than in many other South American countries. There are many female judges, politicians and legislators, and women are becoming more active and assertive in business.

- Venezuelan women are beautiful and work hard on looking great. They want to have heads turn. Even professional women "dress to impress."

- North American businesswomen can operate effectively in Venezuela. Be polite and friendly, but be firm.

- Blondes (*catira*) are pursued with interest.

- Irene Saez, a former Miss Universe, has become the mayor of a municipality, Chacao, which forms part of the city of Caracas, and is respected for running one of the best governments in the country. She is currently a candidate for president.

ESPECIALLY FOR WOMEN

The status of women is higher in Venezuela than in many other South American countries.

HEALTH AND SAFETY

- Good medical facilities are available in the urban areas. The best facilities are private.

- Malaria and cholera are active in rural areas.

- Drinking bottled water is recommended.

- Traffic is fast and chaotic in larger cities. Beware of motorcyclists, often the most aggressive drivers.

- The crime rate is growing in many cities. Caracas and Maracaibo require extra precautions. Pickpockets are active on public transportation, especially in Caracas. Caracas is not safe at night.

- Do not show valuables, jewelry or cameras. Don't leave expensive items in parked cars or on the beaches.

- Avoid public demonstrations, which may turn violent.

Traffic is fast and chaotic in larger cities.

HOLIDAYS AND FESTIVALS

Do not plan to make a business visit or schedule any appointments during the following holidays or festivals. Be sure to check for the numerous regional and local holidays and festivals.

January	New Year's Day (1)
	Epiphany (6)
February/March	Carnival (the Monday and Tuesday before Ash Wednesday, varies)
March	The Feast of San José; Father's Day (19)
March/April	Holy Thursday (varies)
	Good Friday (varies)
	Easter (varies)
April	Declaration of Independence Day (19)
May	Labor Day (1)
	Feast of the Ascension (8)
June	Battle of Carabobo (24)
July	Independence Day (5)
	Simón Bolívar's Birthday (24)
September	Public Officials' Day (the first Monday)
October	Columbus Day (12)
November	All Saints' Day (1)
December	Feast of the Immaculate Conception (8)
	Christmas (25)

During each holiday, statues of Simón Bolívar are decorated with colorful wreaths.

- Religious holidays are observed by the banking sector in accordance with the following National Banking Council regulations: holidays falling on Tuesday or Wednesday are observed the previous Monday, and those falling on Thursday or Friday are observed the following Monday.

REFERENCES

Acuff, Frank L. *How to do Business with Anyone Anywhere around the World*. New York: Amacom, 1993.

America Online, Traveler's Corner (Keyword: [country name]).

Associated Press News Service. New York.

Axtel, Roger E. *Dos and Taboos of Hosting International Visitors*. New York: Wiley, 1990.

Axtel, Roger E. *Gestures*. New York: Wiley, 1991.

Axtel, Roger E., ed. *Dos and Taboos Around the World*. New York: Wiley, 1990.

Background Notes, United States Department of State Bureau of Public Affairs, Office of Public Communication, 1994.

CIA World Factbook. http://www.odci.gov/cia/publications/nsolo/factbook/samr/htm.

Culturgrams, 1997. Provo, Utah: David M. Kennedy Center for International Studies, Brigham Young University, 1997 ed.

"The Diplomat" Newsletter. Cold Spring Harbor, New York: The Diplomat, 1992.

The Economist World Atlas and Almanac. London: The Economist Books, 1997.

Export Hotline. International Strategies, Inc., 1996.

The New York Times. New York: New York Times Company.

Reuters News Service. New York.

Rossman, Marlene L. *The International Businesswoman of the 90's*. New York: Praeger, 1986.

The Wall Street Journal. New York: Dow Jones & Company, Inc.

Webster's Concise World Atlas. Barnes & Noble Books, 1995.

World Book Encyclopedia. Chicago: World Book, Inc., 1994.

World Trade Magazine. Newport Beach, CA: Taipan Press, Inc.

INDEX